**THE
CALYPSO
COOKBOOK**

THE CALYPSO COOKBOOK

by The
Mad Hatter
CAROL
COLLVER
THURBER

Ashley books inc ●
Box 768 · Port Washington, N. Y. 11050

For Gibbs
With A Heartful Of Love

The Mad Hatter doffs his hat, bows to the waist, and gives multiple thanks to his many West Indian donors and stateside testers.

Published simultaneously in Canada by George J. McLeod, Ltd., 73 Bathurst Street, Toronto, Ontario M5V 2P8

THE CALYPSO COOKBOOK, © Copyright 1974 by The Mad Hatter, Carol Collver Thurber
Library of Congress Number: 73-83918
ISBN: 0-87949-014-4

Address information to Ashley Books, Inc., Box 768, Port Washington, New York 11050

Published by Ashley Books, Inc.
Manufactured in the United States of America

First Edition

TABLE OF CONTENTS

I

THINK MAD

In which I introduce myself

SING CALYPSO IN D'KITCHEN! TROMP ROUN'
      IF YOU WISH
WHENEVER YOU CONCOCTEEN SUCCULENT DISH.
BE YOU UP IN ALASKA OR DOWN TRINIDAD
KEEP HEART FULL OF SONG AND REMEMBER:
              think mad

"*Pense comme un idiot!* THINK MAD! This is the secret
of happiness, *mon cheri.*"

So spoke my French grandfather on the island of St. Barts,
when I was a child of two. And thanks to Grandpere
Antoine's sound advice, I have celebrated ninety-seven
birthdays and enjoyed 35,817 days of life. Lest I forget my
grandfather's counsel, Grandmere Marie embroidered a
sampler for me, and those two simple but meaningful words
now decorate the wall at the foot of my hammock in my
little home in Frenchtown, St. Thomas:

```
✿✿✿✿✿✿✿✿✿✿✿✿✿✿✿✿
✿                ✿
✿   THINK MAD    ✿
✿                ✿
✿✿✿✿✿✿✿✿✿✿✿✿✿✿✿✿
```

I implore you not to confuse me with the British Mad
Hatter, notorious for his rude manners. I am not a Britisher
(unless you want to consider Bluebeard, the Pirate, and Sir
Francis Drake, who was a great-great-great granduncle of my
fourth cousin, Esmeralda Gumblehuff). Nor do I indulge in
Mad Tea Parties. But let me assure you that if I were ever to
take a notion to favor you with one, you would find me a
most gracious host.

7

Although my grandparents were French, my heritage derives from many nationalities. I have among my ingredients a driblet of Dutch, a fleck of African, a nip of Norwegian, a smidgen of Spanish, and a toss of Italian. The one blot on my ancestral escutcheon was the English pirate, Bluebeard. But even he had one thing in common with my illustrious predecessors. He too was a *bon vivant.*

But back to Grandpere Antoine and Grandmere Marie. As you have learned, my grandparents were from the French West Indian island of St. Bartholomew, locally known as St. Barts. They reared me, instilling in me an appreciation of the culinary arts. I never knew my parents. My mother died at childbirth, and my father was lost at sea four months later. Shortly after my sixteenth birthday, my grandparents moved to Frenchtown, St. Thomas, in what are now the United States Virgin Islands. And it is here I have spent my happiest days, with my donkey, Lord Ignoramus, my noisy parrot, Percival, and my knock-kneed, pigeon-toed, cross-eyed cat, Slap Foot Wacky Blacky.

Although to my knowledge I have no American blood, my resemblance to Uncle Sam is by no means a coincidence. The cartoonist had searched the globe for a suitable model: tall, lean, bearded, and above all, distinguished, when to his great good fortune he discovered me.

We both chanced to be vacationing on the British island of St. Kitts, and it was there I posed for his famous cartoon: "Uncle Sam Wants You!" My appearance has in no way changed to this day except, of course, that it has taken on the sheen and patina of age.

It was in honor of the cartoonist that I created one of my masterpieces, the UNCLE SAMBURGER. But we shall come to that in due course. For, as Grandpere Antoine wisely told me, "First Things will take care of themselves. Always remember to put:

LAST THINGS FIRST

And so we begin with desserts, confections, and other frivolities.

8

II

TONY GILCH, IMPOSTER

Multiple delectable purloined desserts

In strictest confidence, it was my grandfather who created all of the recipes now served at the world-famous "Antoine's" in New Orleans. The imposter who stole my grandfather's name, along with his culinary masterpieces, was a shoe salesman from Chicago. His real name was Tony Gilch.*

Grandpere Antoine made the acquaintance of Tony in a shoe store in Chicago, in 1838, when he purchased a pair of gaiters. The color he wanted (mustard green) and the size he needed (13 Triple E) were not in stock. Hence, Grandpere Antoine requested they be ordered and delivered to his hotel.

---

* Like his grandson, Grandpere Antoine suffered from a persecution complex, as well as delusions of grandeur, for it is a known fact that throughout his lifetime he journeyed no further than from his native St. Barts to St. Thomas.

A week later, Tony Gilch personally delivered the gaiters to my grandfather at Mother Mahoney's Family Boarding House. They struck up a friendship and within a month Tony, an apt student and able mimic, had learned to speak fluent French. He had also stolen my grandfather's recipe for *Crepes St. Barts,* now known to the world as *Crepes Suzette.*

Two years later, Tony Gilch, posing under the name of Antoine, opened his restaurant in New Orleans. The rest is history.*

Here is the original recipe, created by my grandfather:

---

* The facts are: Antoine Alciatore, foremerly chef of the Hotel de Noailles, in Marseilles, France, emigrated to the United States and founded "Antoine's" in 1840.

CREPES ST. BARTS

1/2 cup sifted flour
1 egg and 1 egg yolk
1/8 teaspoon salt
5 tablespoons milk
3 tablespoons mango jam
powdered sugar

1) Combine flour, egg, egg yolk, salt and milk. Beat until smooth. If necessary, add more milk to make batter the consistency of light cream. Cover and chill for at least half an hour in the refrigerator.
2) Heat a heavy iron frying pan and grease with a paper towel dipped in butter or margarine. Pour in enough batter to barely cover bottom of the pan, tipping it as you add the batter. Brown pancakes on both sides.
3) Remove from pan with a spatula and spread with a thin layer of mango jam. Roll up jelly roll fashion, and sprinkle with powdered sugar.
4) Place under broiler to glaze.

MANGO JAM

2 cups finely chopped mango
1 teaspoon fresh grated, or 1/4
    teaspoon powdered gin-
    ger
juice of 1 lime or lemon
2 cups sugar
water to cover

Place ingredients in a kettle and simmer until jam has thickened, stirring frequently.

As mangos are not plentiful an New Orleans, Tony Gilch substituted currant or red raspberry jelly.

The following are Grandpère Antoine's delectable dessert recipes, most of which were purloined by Tony Gilch:

RHUM BABA

2 cups sifted flour
1 package yeast
1/4 cup warm milk
3 eggs
1/3 cup melted butter
1 1/2 tablespoons sugar
1/2 teaspoon salt

1) Place sifted flour in a mixing bowl, and make a hollow in the center.
2) Soften yeast in warm milk and pour into hollow.
3) Cover and allow to stand 5 minutes.
4) Add eggs one at a time and mix with spoon for 5 minutes.
5) Cover and let dough stand for 30 minutes.
6) Melt and cool the butter, and add sugar and salt.
7) Add to dough and mix or knead until well blended. About 5 minutes.
8) Put into buttered tube pan or cup cake molds. Allow to rise to twice its bulk. About 30 minutes.
9) Bake in preheated oven at 350° for about 20 minutes.
10) Remove from molds and cool on a cake rack. Now they can be wrapped in foil and frozen.
11) Several hours before serving, marinate in hot rum sauce. Serve with a pitcher of remaining sauce.

RUM SAUCE

1 cup water
1 cup sugar
3 slices lime
1 slice orange
1 clove
$1/2$ cup rum

1) Bring all ingredients except rum to a boil, stirring until sugar has dissolved. Simmer 5 minutes.
2) Strain and add rum.

FLOATING VIRGINS

2 cups milk
3 eggs
$1/3$ cup sugar
   pinch of salt
1 tablespoon bourbon
2 tablespoons guava or red
   currant jelly
   sprinkle of ground nutmeg

1) Heat milk in double boiler.
2) Beat 2 egg yolks and 1 whole egg slightly. Add sugar, pinch of salt, then scalded milk, stirring constantly. Forget the beach. Stay with it!

3) When thickened, splash in the bourbon and sprinkle on the nutmeg. Chill.
4) Beat 2 egg whites with jelly until very stiff.
5) Drop by spoonfuls onto chilled custard.

BANANITOS

2 ripe bananas
1 egg
1/2 cup milk
1/2 cup flour
1 teaspoon baking powder
raw honey, mint leaves and
fresh pineapple

1) Mash bananas.
2) Beat in egg.
3) Add milk, and flour combined with baking powder, mixing well.
4) Pour onto greased griddle and brown on both sides. Drizzle with raw honey and garnish with mint leaves and fresh pineapple.
Makes about 16 fritters.

HONEY PLANTAINS

1) Cut plantains in half lengthwise.
2) Sauté in butter.
3) Drizzle honey over each plantain and cook until honey forms a syrup.
Serve hot.

BAKED BANANAS

6 bananas
1/2 cup dark brown sugar
4 tablespoons rum
butter

1) Grease a pie dish thickly with butter. Slice bananas lengthwise and layer alternately with the sugar, topping with sugar.
2) Sprinkle with rum and dot with butter.
3) Bake in a preheated 400° oven for 20 minutes. Serve hot.

MANGO PUDDING

1 egg
2/3 cup sugar
1 tablespoon flour
1 1/4 teaspoons baking powder
1/8 teaspoon salt
1/2 cup chopped nuts
1/2 cup chopped mangos (or
    substitute peaches)
1 teaspoon vanilla

1) Beat egg and sugar together until very smooth. Combine
flour, baking powder and salt. Stir into egg mixture.
2) Add remaining ingredients and bake in a greased pie
pan for 35 minutes at 350°.
4 servings.

SMASHED MAMMEES*

4 mammee apples, mashed
1/2 teaspoon salt
2 teaspoons lime juice
1/2 cup butter
3/4 cup flour
1 teaspoon ground cinnamon
1 teaspoon ground cloves
1/2 cup brown sugar

1) Butter a shallow baking dish and put in the mashed
mammee apples.
2) Sprinkle with salt and lime juice.
3) Blend in butter, flour, brown sugar and spices until
mixture is crumbly. Spread over the mammee apples.
4) Bake uncovered for one hour, in a 350° oven.
4 to 6 servings.

MANGO-PANGO CAKE

3 medium-sized mangos, or 1
    pound, 13 ounce can
    apricots
1/2 cup brown sugar
1/2 cup flour
1/4 teaspoon salt
1/4 teaspoon cinnamon
1/4 cup butter

*Now about those mammee apples: they're grayish, mushy and quite
tasteless, but we St. Thomians pretend we enjoy eating them. Any fruit of
your choice would greatly improve this sentimental recipe.

1) Grease a 9-inch pie plate and spread with mangos.
2) Mix brown sugar, flour, salt and cinnamon. Blend in butter with a fork until mixture is crumbly. Sprinkle over mangos.
3) Bake in preheated 425° oven 15 or 20 minutes, until crumbs are golden brown.

BANGO-PANGO PUDDING

2 ripe bananas
1 egg
1/2 cup sugar
1 cup milk
1 teaspoon vanilla
1 teaspoon butter
1 tablespoon chopped nuts
1 tablespoon grated coconut
1/4 teaspoon cinnamon
1 1/2 teaspoons baking powder

1) Mash bananas and beat until light and fluffy.
2) Beat egg and gradually stir in sugar and milk.
3) Mix in vanilla, butter and bananas.
4) Add flour mixed with baking powder, cinnamon, nuts and coconuts and blend well.
5) Pour into greased pudding mold or double boiler top, grease lid and cover tightly.
6) Set over boiling water and steam until pudding leaves sides of mold. About 1 hour.

COCONUT PIE (makes own crust)

4 eggs, well beaten
1 cup sugar
1 cup grated coconut
1/4 teaspoon salt
1 teaspoon vanilla
2 cups milk
1/4 cup butter, melted
1/2 cup flour
1/2 teaspoon cream of tartar
1/4 teaspoon baking soda

1) To well-beaten eggs add sugar, coconut, vanilla, salt, milk, butter, and flour sifted with cream of tartar and baking soda, and beat to mix well.
2) Pour into a greased deep 10-inch pie pan and bake at 350° for 50 minutes, or until brown, and a sea egg spine or toothpick stabbed into center comes out dry.

14

LIME FLUFF PUFFS
The Puffs

1 cup water
1/2 cup butter or margarine
1/4 teaspoon salt
1 cup sifted flour
4 eggs

1) Combine water, butter and salt in a saucepan and bring to boiling point.
2) Add flour all at once and stir rapidly until mixture leaves sides of pan and forms a ball.
3) Cook about 3 minutes longer, mashing dough with spoon against sides of pan.
4) Remove from heat and beat about 2 minutes to cool mixture slightly.
5) Add eggs one at a time, beating thoroughly.
6) Continue beating until mixture is smooth.
7) Pick up rounded tablespoon of dough with one spoon and scrape it onto an ungreased baking sheet with a second spoon.
8) Swirl top and avoid leaving peaks at surface.
9) Place mounds 2 inches apart and bake at 450° for 15 minutes, then at 325° 5 or 10 minutes longer. Watch them!
10) Remove from oven. Cut slit into each puff and return to oven about 5 minutes longer.
11) Remove to rack and cool.
   Makes 10 to 12 medium to large puffs.

The Fluff

4 eggs, separated
1 tablespoon gelatin
3 tablespoons water
1/2 cup sugar
1/4 teaspoon grated lime rind
6 tablespoons lime juice

1) Soak gelatin in water.
2) Beat egg yolks, sugar and lime rind until light and fluffy.
3) Add gelatin and half the lime juice and cook in double boiler, stirring until gelatin is dissolved.
4) Add remaining juice and stir lime mixture into egg yolk mixture.
5) Fold into stiffly beaten egg whites.
6) Slit puffs and spoon lime fluff into them.

COCONUT RHUMBA

1 cup grated coconut
3 eggs
3 tablespoons rum
1/2 cup sugar
2 cups cream (1/2 and 1/2)
   generous pinch each: nut-
      meg and salt
1/4 cup toasted chopped pecans

1) Beat eggs and sugar over a pan of boiling water until thick.
2) Fold in coconut and remaining ingredients.
3) Dump into a buttered casserole, or custard cups. Set in a panful of water and bake at 350° for 40 to 45 minutes.
4) Sprinkle with toasted pecans just before serving.

GUAVA PIE

3 cups peeled and sliced
   guavas
2 tablespoons sugar
1 tablespoon lime juice

1) Wash and peel guavas, removing pulp and seeds.
2) Slice guavas and place in saucepan with sugar, lime juice and a little water. Simmer until fruit is tender.
3) Line a shallow pie plate with pastry and fill with cooked guavas.
4) Top with remaining pastry and make slits to allow steam to escape.
5) Bake in hot oven until brown.

Short Crust Pastry

2 cups flour
1/2 teaspoon salt
1 teaspoon baking powder
1/3 cup margarine
1/3 cup lard
1/3 cup ice water

1) Sift flour, salt and baking powder into a mixing bowl.
2) Cut shortening into flour mixture with a knife, until crumbly.
3) Sprinkle with ice water and, still using a knife, mix into dough.
4) Lay pastry on a floured board and roll lightly from center outwards.

16

LIME MERINGUE PIE

6 tablespoons flour
3/4 cups sugar
   pinch of salt
1 cup water
1/2 cup lime juice
1/2 teaspoon grated lime rind
   green food coloring
3 eggs
3 tablespoons butter or mar-
    garine
3 tablespoons sugar
   9-inch baked pie shell
   Short Crust Pastry above

1) Mix flour, sugar and salt to a smooth paste with a little of the water, gradually adding the remaining water, lime juice and rind.
2) Tint with a *soupcon* of green coloring.
3) Cook in double boiler, stirring until thick.
4) Beat egg yolks and gradually add hot mixture, stirring constantly.
5) Pour mixture back into pan and cook about 7 minutes.
6) Add butter and pour into baked pastry shell.
7) Beat egg whites until stiff. Add 3 tablespoons sugar gradually.
8) Pile on filling and bake at 350° until golden. (About 10 minutes)

RUM PIE

3 tablespoons rum
2 tablespoons water
1/4 cup sugar
2 teaspoons gelatin
3 egg yolks
1 cup heavy cream, lightly
   whipped
1/4 cup coarsely grated chocolate
   Short Crust Pastry

1) Press pastry evenly on bottom and sides of a 9-inch pie plate, using the back of a spoon.
2) Bake at 350° for 10 minutes.
3) Cool.
4) Place gelatin and 2 tablespoons water in a small bowl and heat over a pan of hot water until dissolved. Allow to cool slightly.

5) Beat egg yolks and sugar until thick and fluffy. Stir in rum and gelatin.
6) Chill until set (2 to 3 hours).
7) Garnish with grated chocolate.
   6 lusty servings.

LEMONADE PIE

1 cup evaporated milk
1 tablespoon unflavored gelatin
¹/₄ cup cold water
¹/₂ cup boiling water
²/₃ cup sugar
1 6-ounce can frozen lemonade concentrate
1 teaspoon grated lemon rind

1) Chill evaporated milk in ice tray until almost frozen around edges.
2) Soften gelatin in cold water in a 3-quart bowl.
3) Add ¹/₂ cup boiling water. Stir until gelatin is dissolved.
4) Stir in sugar and lemonade concentrate and continue stirring. Add grated lemon rind and keep on with that stirring. Chill.
5) In a 1-quart bowl whip ice cold milk until stiff. Fold into chilled gelatin mixture.
6) Pile into 9-inch pie pan lined with graham cracker crust. Chill until firm. Can also be frozen.

GRAHAM CRACKER CRUST

³/₄ cup graham cracker crumbs
¹/₂ cup wheat germ
2 tablespoons sugar
¹/₄ cup melted butter or margarine

1) Combine graham cracker crumbs, wheat germ, sugar and melted butter in a bowl. Stir well to blend.
2) Remove and set aside 2 tablespoons for garnish.
3) Press remaining crumb mixture on bottom and sides of a 9-inch pie plate.
4) Bake at 350° about 5 minutes. Cool. Then fill with lemonade pie mixture and sprinkle with reserved crumbs.
5) Chill at least 3 hours before serving. Or freeze and serve a month from now.

PEANUT BUTTER FLUFF PIE

 1 envelope unflavored gelatin
1/4 cup sugar
1/4 teaspoon salt
 1 cup milk
 2 eggs, separated
1/2 cup crunchy peanut butter
1/4 cup brown sugar, packed
 1 teaspoon vanilla
 1 cup heavy cream
 1 baked 9-inch pie shell
 1 tablespoon sugar
   chocolate curls

1) Combine gelatin, sugar and salt. Add milk, slightly beaten egg yolks and peanut butter.
2) Stir over moderate heat until gelatin is dissolved and custard smooth.
3) Remove from heat and chill.
4) Beat egg whites until foamy. Stir in brown sugar, a little at a time, and beat until stiff.
5) Fold whites into peanut butter mixture and add vanilla.
6) Whip cream until stiff and fold half of it into filling.
7) Spoon into crust.
8) Chill until firm.
9) Just before serving, fold 1 tablespoon sugar into remaining whipped cream and spread over pie.
10) Garnish with chocolate curls.

TAMARINDS IN SYRUP

Remove pods and sprinkle tamarinds with brown sugar and lime juice. Place in sun for 2 days.

STEWED MAMMEE APPLE

 1 large mammee
 1 cup sugar
 3 cloves
 2 teaspoons lime juice
1/4 teaspoon salt
1/4 teaspoon ground cinnamon
 2 cups water

Blend all ingredients and chill for 3 or 4 hours or overnight. Stew for 10 or 15 minutes. Chill again.

GENIP SIPPER

2 quarts genips
2 quarts boiling water
sugar to taste

1) Pop fruit from its leathery green skin and cover with boiling water.
2) Allow to stand 3 hours.
3) Stir, strain and add sugar to taste. Chill 3 or 4 hours.

ESPRESSO COFFEE JELLY

1 tablespoon (or one enve-
    lope) unflavored gelatin
2 cups cold water
$1/2$ cup sugar
$1/8$ teaspoon salt
1 tablespoon instant Espresso
    coffee
$1^1/2$ tablespoons lime or lemon
    juice
$1/4$ teaspoon nutmeg

1) Sprinkle gelatin on $1/2$ cup cold water in saucepan to soften. Place over medium heat.
2) Stir constantly until gelatin is dissolved.
3) Remove from heat and add sugar, salt, Espresso and lime juice.
4) Stir until sugar is dissolved and add remaining $1^1/2$ cups water.
5) Chill until thickened, then stir in nutmeg.
6) Turn into 4 iced frappe glasses and chill until firm. Squirt on some whipped cream.
    4 servings.

III

A MAD CHEF IS BORN

Psychedelic Psundaes and Enticing Ices

No doubt you marvel at my command of English. In all modesty, I must confess to marvelling at it myself, considering my upbringing on St. Barts and, subsequently, the sounds that have accosted my eardrums on St. Thomas. "Calypso" English, on the one hand, and the French patois of my Frenchtown neighbors, on the other.

But let me explain my mastery of English. At the age of sixteen, determined to better myself, I left St. Thomas as a stowaway on a three-masted schooner destined for San Juan and, upon arrival, jumped ship and enrolled as an English major at the University of Puerto Rico. Being poverty stricken, I did the only logical thing. I established an ice cream booth on campus and, years ahead of my time as always, created the Psychedelic Psundae.

My ice cream creation became such a craze among my fellow students that I moved to larger quarters on the plaza. I prospered, and soon I no longer had room for the dollars beneath my mattress. Hence I invested in a safe, and have ever since contended:

BETTER PSAFE THAN PSORRY

The following is my renowned recipe:

21

PSYCHEDELIC PSUNDAE
Banana Ice Cream

4 ripe bananas, crushed (1½
    cups)
½ cup sugar
⅔ cup light corn syrup
⅓ cup orange juice
⅓ cup lemon juice
1 large can evaporated milk
    (2 cups)

1) Combine first 5 ingredients and marinate until sugar has dissolved.
2) Add milk and freeze in 2 ice cube trays.

Psundae

For my original creation I made use of local fruits: guava-berries, mammees, soursops, genips, sopadillas and tamarinds. I now use modern food coloring and flavors, which are just as effective. You will need:

red, yellow and green food
    coloring
3 sea egg spines, or tooth-
    picks
chocolate chips, shredded
    coconut, cake decorators,
    snips of maraschino cher-
    ry, nuts, or what-else-
    have-you-on-the-shelf

1) Scoop out banana ice cream and shape into balls.
2) Dip a toothpick in red food coloring and smear on ice cream. Repeat, using a fresh toothpick for each color. Make it wild!
3) Sprinkle with any of the above ingredients you fancy, the madder, the better, but be sure to have these lined up before you remove ice cream from the freezer, and work fast. Otherwise you will have a Psloppy Psychedelic Psundae.
4) Wrap each ball in plastic wrap and store in freezer until you're ready for a psychedelic party.
8 servings.

And here are more of my ice cream booth recipes:

LIME WHOOP

3/4 cup sugar
1 1/2 teaspoons gelatin
1 1/2 cups water
1/4 cup lime juice
1 teaspoon grated lime rind
2 stiffly beaten egg whites

1) Blend sugar and gelatin in double boiler.
2) Add water and stir over low heat until gelatin dissolves.
3) Cool, and add lime juice and rind.
4) Pour into freezer tray and freeze until mushy.
5) Remove and beat in chilled bowl. Fold in beaten egg whites and freeze until firm.
   4 to 6 servings.

COINTREAU SHERBET

2 teaspoons gelatin
3/4 cup cold water
3/4 cup sugar
1/2 cup cointreau
1 cup orange juice
1 tablespoon lime juice
pinch of salt

1) Soften gelatin in 1/4 cup water.
2) Combine remaining water and sugar, and boil 1 minute.
3) Add gelatin and stir until dissolved.
4) Add remaining ingredients and cool.
5) Pour into freezer tray and freeze until firm around the edges.
6) Pour into a chilled bowl and beat until smooth.
   Return to tray and freeze until firm.

CHOCOLATE COCONUT BALLS

1) Shape chocolate ice cream into balls with ice cream scoop.
2) Roll in shredded coconut and freeze quickly on a flat tray.
3) When firm, wrap each ball in foil until serving time.

MANGO ICE CREAM

2 pounds mangos
2 tablespoons lime juice
2 tablespoons confectioners
    sugar
1½ cups granulated sugar
1 cup heavy cream
2 eggs, separated

1) Remove fruit from pit, sprinkle with lime juice and crush.
2) Add sugar and mix well.
3) Beat egg whites with confectioners sugar until stiff.
4) Beat egg yolks and fold gently into egg whites.
5) Whip cream and fold into egg mixture.
6) Fold in mangos and pour into freezer trays.
7) Freeze until firm around edges.
8) Transfer to a chilled bowl and beat until smooth.
9) Freeze until firm.

SOURSOP ICE CREAM

1 large soursop
1½ cups boiling water
1 cup condensed milk
1 cup evaporated milk

1) Wash and peel soursop.
2) Mash pulp and pour boiling water over it.
3) Let stand until cool, then strain, squeezing well to get out all the juice.
4) Mix juice with condensed milk.
5) Whip evaporated milk and combine the two.
6) Freeze until mushy. Then remove from freezer and beat until smooth.
7) Return to freezer until set.

BUTTERMILK SHERBET

2 cups buttermilk
¼ teaspoon ginger powder
½ cup sugar
1 cup crushed pineapple
1 teaspoon shredded coconut.
1 egg white

1) Combine all but egg white and pour into freezer trays until mushy.
2) Add 1 egg white and beat until frothy, in chilled bowl.
3) Pour back into freezer trays and freeze until firm, stirring frequently.

MAD MANDARINS

1 3-ounce package lime gelatin
3/4 cup hot water
1 6-ounce can frozen orange
   juice
1 pint vanilla ice cream
1/2 teaspoon fresh ginger root,
   grated, or a pinch of
   powdered ginger
1 11-ounce can mandarin
   oranges, drained

1) Dissolve gelatin in water and add frozen orange juice and ginger.
2) Let ice cream stand at room temperature until soft enough to stir.
3) Combine with gelatin mixture.
4) Add mandarin oranges, reserving 4 sections, and pour into a 1 quart mold.
5) Chill several hours, or overnight, then garnish with reserved mandarin sections.

MANGO MELBA

3 mangos, or 4 large peaches
1/2 cup guava or red currant
   jelly
1 10-ounce package frozen
   raspberries, thawed
1/4 cup dark rum
1 quart vanilla ice cream
   whipped cream

1) Wash and peel mangos.
2) Mix jelly and raspberries with rum and pour over mangos.
3) Refrigerate several hours.
4) At serving time, divide mangos into 6 dessert dishes. Scoop ice cream on top. Cover with raspberry-guava sauce and top with whipped cream.

PAPAYA SUNDAE

1 medium papaya, peeled
    and crushed
2 teaspoons lime juice
1 teaspoon ginger root, sliv-
    ered
1 teaspoon lime rind, grated
1 tablespoon chopped coco-
    nut

1) Combine above and refrigerate several hours.
2) Divide 1 quart vanilla ice cream into 6 serving dishes and top with sauce.

PINEAPPLE COOL-OFF

3 eggs, separated
  pinch of salt
$1/8$ teaspoon powdered ginger
$1/2$ cup sugar
 1 9-ounce can crushed pi-
    neapple
2 tablespoons lime juice
2 tablespoons sugar
1 cup heavy cream

1) Beat egg yolks with salt and ginger.
2) Add $1/2$ cup sugar and beat until smooth.
3) Drain pineapple and mix with lime juice.
4) Blend into egg and sugar mixture and heat in double boiler, stirring until spoon is coated.
5) Stir in pineapple and transfer to mixing bowl to cool.
6) Beat egg whites until stiff, then fold in remaining 2 tablespoons of sugar until smooth.
7) Whip cream. Fold cream and then egg white into pineapple mixture.
8) Pour into 2 freezer trays and freeze until firm around the edges.
9) Remove from freezer, break up with a spoon, and return to freezer.

GINGER LIME SHERBET

2 egg whites
$1/4$ cup sugar
1 cup corn syrup
$1/2$ teaspoon grated ginger root
    or $1/4$ teaspoon powdered
    ginger

2 cups milk
2/3 cup lime juice
1/2 teaspoon grated lime rind

1) Beat egg whites until stiff.
2) Gradually fold in sugar and add corn syrup, milk, lime rind, juice and ginger.
3) Pour into freezer tray and freeze until almost firm.
4) Pour into chilled bowl and beat until smooth.
5) Return to tray and freeze until firm.

FROZEN APRICOT MOUSSE

1 cup cooked, sweetened
    dried apricots
2 eggs
1/2 teaspoon vanilla
    pinch of salt
1/3 cup sugar
1 cup heavy cream, beaten
    stiff

1) Mash apricots.
2) Beat eggs until light and fluffy and fold in the sugar gradually.
3) Combine with apricots, vanilla and salt, and fold in cream.
4) Turn into freezer trays and freeze until almost firm.
5) Pour into chilled bowl and beat until smooth.
6) Return to tray and freeze until firm.

IV

CHA! CHA! HA! HA!

Cha Cha Hats and Sand Dollahs:

Pierre Le Duc's Cookies and Cakes

"CHA CHA! HA HA! HA HA!"

The singsong squawking of Percival, my parrot, is an everlasting reminder of the ridicule to which my grandparents were subjected when they moved to St. Thomas. To the outrage of Grandpère Antoine and the other early settlers from St. Barts, their little fishing village of Frenchtown on the harbor was looked down upon by the natives, who laughingly called it "Cha Cha Town."

According to my grandfather, the term "Cha Cha" derives from a fish so small it's good for nothing—a *"rien de tout."* But St. Thomians have a different version, claiming the French fishermen were such hard bargainers that when purchasers tried to bid them down on the price of their fish they would mutter, "Cha cha," meaning, "No deal."

Grandpère Antoine and his fellow settlers were infuriated by the name for, like my contemporaries in Frenchtown today, they were hard-working fishermen and industrious weavers of straw. They wore somber clothes and their tall straw hats, woven of palm fronds imported from St. Barts, were decorated with nothing other than an austere black band.

Along with my grandfather's parrot, Percival, I inherited his resentment of the derogatory name until one day, as I lay in my hammock putting the finishing touches on a tall straw hat, I chanced to glance up at my sampler, which reminded me to:

❖❖❖❖❖❖❖❖❖❖❖❖❖❖
❖   ❖
❖ THINK MAD ❖
❖   ❖
❖❖❖❖❖❖❖❖❖❖❖❖❖❖

At just that moment, Percival blasted:

"CHA CHA! HA HA! CHA CHA! HA HA!"

Lord Ignoramus brayed at the squawking, and Slap Foot Wacky Blacky awoke from her usual all-day nap and stretched.

Suddenly my brain clicked into focus. Why not turn ridicule to advantage?

Make a *Cha Cha Hat*.

I quickly ripped off the traditional black band from the hat I was making and replaced it with a flashy red ribbon with yellow polka dots. I then decorated it with every brightly colored straw object I could lay my hands on: green donkeys, orange pelicans, purple fish, crowning the *Cha Cha Chapeau* with fresh hibiscus blossoms from my garden.

Thus the famous *"Cha Cha Hat"* was created—a hat so popular with tourists and St. Thomians alike that I and my neighbors of Frenchtown now have the last laugh. As Sir Francis Bacon once said (in strictest confidence) to my great-great-great-great grand-uncle Molière:

And so it ensued that my Frenchtown neighbor, Pierre Le Duc, was inspired to create his recipe for:

CHA CHA HATS

Oatmeal Cooky Brims

$^1/_2$ **cup butter**
$^1/_2$ **cup white sugar**
$^1/_2$ **cup brown sugar, firmly packed**
  1 **egg**
  1 **cup all purpose flour**
  1 **cup oatmeal**
$^1/_2$ **teaspoon soda**
$^1/_4$ **teaspoon baking powder**
$^1/_4$ **teaspoon salt**
$^1/_2$ **teaspoon cinnamon**

¼ teaspoon nutmeg
½ teaspoon vanilla
½ cup raisins
½ cup chopped nuts

1) Cream butter and sugar, then add egg and all other ingredients, stirring fiendishly. Drop by spoonfuls 2 inches apart on cooky sheet.
2) Bake at 350° about 15 minutes.
3) While these are cooling, make the

Cha Cha Frosting

½ cup butter or margarine
1 cup granulated sugar
¼ cup milk
1 teaspoon vanilla extract
1½ to 2 cups sifted confection-
    ers sugar

1) Melt butter in saucepan.
2) Add granulated sugar, milk and vanilla. Stir until blended. Bring to a boil, stirring occasionally.
3) Cool. Then gradually add confectioners sugar until thick enough to spread, beating well after each addition.
4) Separate into 3 bowls, and add red, yellow and green food coloring—one color for each bowl.

The Crowning Touch

1) Frost cookies and crown each with a marshmallow.
2) Remembering to THINK MAD, smear marshmallows with the colored frosting.

Pierre Le Duc is a known character on St. Thomas. He often walks to Magens Bay—a long hike across the town of Charlotte Amalie and up and over the mountains. But Pierre has a purpose. He collects sand dollars.

Upon his return home he lolls in his hammock and, one by one, tosses the sand dollars out the window over the oleander bushes and into the sea. This of course is bewildering to any passer-by who does not know his objective. Whenever anyone stops to ask him why he tosses sand dollars, one by one, out the window over the oleander bushes and into the sea, the answer they receive is terse:

"To keep the elephants away."

"But there aren't any elephants on St. Thomas!"

Pierre Le Duc sighs. "Indeed not, *monsieur! Voila!* You see how effective my method is?"

There are days when Pierre just wants to relax in his hammock, enjoying the gentle Trade Winds and sipping a cool limeade. On such days he substitutes a simple cooky of his invention, which he claims serves the same purpose.

PIERRE LE DUC'S SAND DOLLAHS

¹/₂ cup butter
1 cup white sugar
2 eggs
1¹/₂ tablespoons milk
2 cups all purpose flour
1¹/₂ teaspoons baking powder
pinch of salt
¹/₂ teaspoon nutmeg
¹/₂ teaspoon vanilla extract
slivered almonds

1) Cream butter and sugar, add eggs and other ingredients. Mix well.
2) Drop teaspoons of mixture on cooky sheet, flattening with buttered glass, dipped in sugar.
3) Make pattern below by pressing in almond slivers.
4) Bake in a preheated 425° oven about 12 minutes.

In strictest secrecy, Pierre Le Duc has presented me with his other recipes for cookies and cake, which I am pleased to share with you.

COCONIBBLES

1 cup sifted flour
1 teaspoon baking powder
¹/₂ teaspoon salt
1 cup brown sugar
¹/₄ cup butter
1 egg
1 tablespoon chopped nuts
1 tablespoon rum
1 cup quick cooking oatmeal
1¹/₂ cups ground coconut

31

1) Cream butter and sugar, add beaten egg and other ingredients.
2) Drop by teaspoonful onto greased cooky sheet and flatten with spoon.
3) Bake at 400° for 15 minutes, or until golden brown.

HONEYS

      1 cup butter
      1 egg
   1/2 cup sugar
      4 tablespoons raw-wild honey
2 1/2 cups sifted flour
   1/8 teaspoon salt
   1/4 cup chopped nuts (optional)

1) Cream butter, sugar and raw-wild honey.
2) Stir in flour, salt, lightly beaten egg and nuts.
3) Chill for 2 hours.
4) Roll out on wax paper to about 1/2 inch thickness. Cut in squares.
5) Bake at 400° for 12 to 15 minutes.

SINFULLY RICH BROWNIES

      2 eggs
   1/2 cup cocoa or 2 squares melted chocolate
1 1/2 cups brown sugar
   1/2 cup sifted flour
   1/4 teaspoon salt
   3/4 cups ground coconut
   1/2 teaspoon vanilla extract

1) Beat eggs, add remaining ingredients. Pour into greased 9 inch square cake pan. Spread with wet spatula.
2) Bake at 350° for 20 minutes. Cut into squares while hot.

SHOW OFFS
(Cheese Cake Cookies)

   1/3 cup butter or margarine
   1/3 cup firmly packed brown sugar
      1 cup flour
   1/4 cup white sugar
      1 8-ounce package cream cheese

¹/₂ cup finely chopped walnuts
  1 egg
  1 tablespoon milk
  1 tablespoon lime or lemon
     juice
 ¹/₂ teaspoon vanilla extract

1) Cream butter with brown sugar
2) Add flour and walnuts and mix to make a crumb mixture. Save one cup for the topping. Press remainder into bottom of an 8 inch square pan.
3) Bake in a preheated 350° oven for 12 to 15 minutes until light brown.
4) Blend sugar with cream cheese until smooth. Add egg, milk, lime and vanilla. Beat well and spread over crust.
5) Sprinkle with crumb mixture and bake at 350° for 25 minutes. Cool and cut into 16 2-inch squares.

COCOROONS

  2 cups grated coconut
 ³/₄ cup sugar
  1
    egg white
 ¹/₄ teaspoon nutmeg
  1 teaspoon sherry
    pinch of salt

1) Mix all ingredients and form into a stiff paste with egg white.
2) Roll into balls the size of a booby bird's egg.
3) Place on greased cooky sheet and bake in a preheated 350° oven until light brown. About 20 minutes.

MANGO TARTS

 ¹/₄ pound butter
  1 cup sugar
  2 eggs
  2 teaspoons rum
 ²/₃ cup rice flour
    mango jam,* or any other
      jam of your choice

1) Line tart pans or small muffin pans with pastry**.
2) Place a teaspoon of jam in the bottom of each.
3) Combine butter, sugar, eggs, rum and rice flour.
4) Mix well and pour into tart shells.
5) Bake in a preheated 425° oven for 15 minutes.
6) Let set 5 to 10 minutes before removing from tins. Makes about 30 tarts.

FISHIES

1 cup butter or margarine
1 8-ounce can almond paste
³/₄ cup sugar
1 egg
3 cups unsifted flour

1) Beat together the butter,
   almond paste and sugar until creamy.
2) Add egg and gradually mix in the flour until thoroughly
   blended.
3) Shape into fish:

4) Bake on an ungreased cooky sheet in a preheated 325°
   oven for about 20 minutes, or until lightly browned.
   (Time will vary according to size.)

LIME SKINNIES

1 cup butter
2 cups sugar
3 tablespoons lime juice
3 cups flour
3 eggs, well beaten

1) Cream butter and sugar. Blend in eggs.
2) Add lime juice and flour. Mix well and chill at least an
   hour.
3) Roll out ¹/₈ inch thick. Cut into squares and bake at 400°
   for 12 to 15 minutes.

PUDDING COOKIES

1 package vanilla or choco-
    late pudding
1 cup all-purpose biscuit mix
1/4 cup shortening
1 egg
3 tablespoons milk
1/2 cup chocolate chips

1) Combine pudding mix and biscuit mix. Cut in shortening until mixture resembles coarse meal.
2) Add egg and milk, blending well. Stir in chocolate chips.
3) Drop dough from teaspoon onto ungreased baking sheet.
4) Bake in a preheated 375° oven for 10 to 12 minutes, or until lightly browned.
Makes about 2 dozen cookies

BANANA CAKE

1/2 cup shortening
1 cup sugar
2 eggs, well beaten
1 cup mashed ripe bananas
1 teaspoon grated orange
    rind
2 cups sifted flour
1 1/4 teaspoons baking powder
1/4 teaspoon baking soda
1/2 teaspoon salt
1/4 cup sour milk
1/2 teaspoon vanilla extract

1) Cream shortening and sugar. Add eggs and beat well. Mix in bananas, orange rind and vanilla.
2) Add combined dry ingredients alternately with the milk, mixing well after each addition.
3) Grease a 9-inch square pan. Pour in mixture and bake in a preheated 350° oven for 50 to 55 minutes.

GINGER CAKE

1 cup molasses
1/2 cup boiling water
2 1/2 cups flour
1 teaspoon soda
1 teaspoon fresh ginger root,
    grated, or
2 teaspoons powdered ginger

1) Add water to molasses.
2) Mix and sift dry ingredients.
3) Combine mixtures and beat vigorously.
4) Pour into buttered shallow pan.
5) Bake in a preheated 350° oven for 30 minutes.

GINGERSNAP CHEESE CAKE

1 3-ounce package cream
    cheese
12 maraschino cherries
1/2 cup chopped walnuts
16 gingersnaps

1) Break up cheese and beat until soft.
2) Cut cherries with wet scissors and chop nuts. Stir into softened cheese.
3) For each portion, put 4 crumbled gingersnaps together and place in layers alternately with cheese cake mixture.
4) Chill for at least 3 hours.

APPLE SAUCE CAKE

2 slices stale white
    bread
2 tablespoons butter
2 tablespoons sugar
1 teaspoon powdered cinna-
    mon
2 cups apple sauce
    whipped cream
1/4 teaspoon powdered cloves

1) Crush bread into crumbs.
2) Melt butter and add to crumbs, blending with a fork.
3) Add sugar, cloves and cinnamon powder, and stir mixture gently until crisp.
4) Divide into 4 dessert dishes and pack down with fork.
5) Place a tablespoon or more applesauce on crumb crust and top with whipped cream.

UPSIDE DOWN MANGO CAKES

1 cup sliced mangos, or
    peaches
1/2 cup firmly packed brown
    sugar

1/4 cup butter or margarine
3 tablespoons water
2 tablespoons chopped nuts
8 maraschino cherries

1) Place brown sugar, butter and water in a 9-inch cake pan and stir until sugar is dissolved, and butter melted.
2) Arrange mangos, nuts and cherries on top of sugar mixture. Top with:

SEA FOAM CAKE

2 egg yolks
1 cup sugar
3/8 cup hot water
1 teaspoon lime juice
1/2 teaspoon lime rind, grated
2 egg whites, beaten stiff
1 cup flour
1 1/2 teaspoons baking powder
1/4 teaspoon salt

1) Preheat oven to 350°.
2) Beat egg yolks until thick and add half the sugar gradually.
3) Continue beating, then add water, remaining sugar, lime juice, rind and egg whites.
4) Sift flour with baking powder and salt. Fold into above mixture.
5) Bake 25 or 30 minutes, or until sea egg spine or toothpick comes out dry.

MUDPIE CAKE

1 1/2 cups sifted flour
4 tablespoons cocoa
1 teaspoon soda
1 cup brown sugar
1/2 teaspoon salt
5 tablespoons vegetable oil
1 tablespoon lime or lemon
    juice
1 teaspoon vanilla extract
1 cup cold water

1) Sift flour, cocoa, soda, sugar and salt into a 9-inch greased square cake pan.
2) Poke holes in mudpie and pour in oil, lime juice and vanilla, then pour cold water over the whole mess.

3) Stir it up and bake in a preheated 300° oven for 40 minutes, or until sea egg spine or toothpick comes out dry.

CARROT CAKE

1¼ cups oil
2 cups sugar
2 teaspoons cinnamon
2 cups flour
1 teaspoon salt
2 teaspoons baking powder
3 cups grated carrots
1 tablespoon baking soda
1 cup finely chopped nuts
4 eggs

1) Cream oil and sugar.
2) Add half of combined dry ingredients.
3) Gradually add remaining ingredients, alternately with eggs, beating well after each addition.
4) Fold in carrots and nuts.
5) Bake in greased tube pan in a preheated 325° oven about an hour.
6) Cool in pan.

LEMON CAKE

1 box yellow cake mix 1 pound 2.5 ounce size
1 3-ounce package lemon jello
4 eggs
¾ cups water
¾ cups oil
1 teaspoon lemon rind

1) Beat the above 2 or 3 minutes until smooth.
2) Pour into greased cake tin and bake in a preheated 350° oven for 40 minutes, or until sea egg spine or toothpick comes out dry.
3) Let cake cool for 5 minutes. Poke holes with fork over the entire cake and pour icing over it.
4) Frost with 2 cups confectioners sugar blended with juice of 2 lemons.

V

THE MAD KING OF MADWICH

Rocking Throne Madwiches

Historians would have us believe that the sandwich was originated by the Earl of Sandwich, a noted gambler. They inform us that, rather than pause for a repast, he ordered chunks of beef or mutton placed between two slices of bread and served to him in the gambling hall.

The little known fact (and my information comes from a secret but reliable source) is that the sandwich was the invention of the Mad King of Madwich, who spent his every waking hour upon his throne—a golden rocking chair designed to conform to his ample proportions. (In fact the king was so fat that behind his back his subjects called him "His Plumpness.") He devoted his life to rocking his throne and weaving butterfly nets.

"We must be prepared," he warned his henchmen. "The butterflies are plotting to overthrow my kingdom. At this very instant, they are probably lurking over our heads on some unknown planet, working out the details for their invasion." He alerted his guards to watch twenty-four hours a day from the towers of his castle.

Meantime, so busy was he weaving butterfly nets that he could not take time from his duties to dine in the royal banquet hall. Hence, he commanded that his beef or mutton be placed between two slices of bread and served to him on a golden tray.

Month after month, and year after year, His Plumpness, the Mad King of Madwich, sat upon his throne, rocking and weaving, rocking and weaving, and munching on madwiches, until suddenly one morning he jumped from his rocker with a blood-curdling yell.

"Grab your nets, men!" he shrieked. "The butterflies have landed!"

Thus having shouted, he ran through the portals of the castle as fast as his chubby legs could carry him. Out into the village square he ran in a wild frenzy, waving his net in the air.

His subjects rushed from every direction to watch his performance. Heads shook, and tongues tut-tutted, for the truth was that only their king could see the butterflies. Word travelled fast, and before sundown the entire populace of the Kingdom of Madwich knew that their king was:

OFF HIS ROCKER!

Through good fortune I have been able to procure the madwich recipes from my above mentioned secret but reliable source.

MANGO CRUNCH

1) Combine ¹/₃ cup mayonnaise, ¹/₃ cup butter or margarine, and ¹/₃ cup softened cream cheese. Blend thoroughly, and store for spreading on any of your madwiches, especially fruity ones.
2) Spread the above on dark bread, then smear on a thin layer of honey.
3) Sprinkle with chopped nuts.
4) Add slices of mango and another sprinkling of nuts. Serve open-faced.

ORANGEY ONIONS

1) Spread bread of your choice with mayonnaise, butter and cream cheese mixture.
2) Slice onions and oranges thin and layer on top.
3) Cover with another slice of bread spread with ¹/₃-¹/₃-¹/₃ mixture.

BANANA DOG

1) Spread hot dog buns with ¹/₃-¹/₃-¹/₃ and warm.
2) Sauté one medium-sized banana in butter or margarine, and sprinkle with minced celery, lime juice and a pinch of salt for each serving.
3) Place in warmed buns and serve fast.

HAM FRAMBLE

¹/₂ cup crushed pineapple
¹/₄ teaspoon ground ginger
 1 teaspoon fresh mint,
     minced
 1 teaspoon butter or margar-
     ine
 1 tablespoon brown sugar
 1 teaspoon sherry
 4 hamburger buns
   prepared mustard
 4 to 8 slices cooked ham
     (depending on size)

1) Simmer pineapple, ginger, mint, butter, brown sugar and
   sherry in a double boiler for 5 minutes.
2) Spread buns with mustard, add ham slices and top with
   pineapple mixture.
3) Bake, open-faced, 10 minutes at 375° until bubbly.
   2 to 4 hearty servings. Or how hungry are you?

BONITA-PAPAYAWICH

 8 slices bread
 1 cup flaked cooked bonita,
     or 1 6¹/₂-ounce can tuna,
     drained
¹/₂ papaya, or 1 large peach,
     peeled
¹/₂ cup mayonnaise
 1 teaspoon lime juice
¹/₂ teaspoon curry powder

1) Blend mayonnaise, lime juice and curry powder, and
   spread evenly over bread.
2) Distribute tuna over 4 slices and add sliced papaya or
   peach.
3) Top with remaining 4 slices of bread.

CHEDDUFINS

 4 English muffins, split
 1 onion, chopped
¹/₃ cup mayonnaise
³/₄ cups grated cheddar
 1 peeled tomato, chopped
¹/₄ teaspoon worcestershire

1) Combine ingredients in mixing bowl.
2) Spread over muffins and toast under broiler until cheese melts.

PINEAPPLE PUFFLE

4 hamburger buns
  butter or margarine
4 slices pineapple
$^1/_4$ cup chopped nuts
4 slices cooked chicken
  breast (Naked Chicken,
  p. 91)
$^1/_3$ cup mayonnaise
$^1/_4$ cup chopped celery
  pinch of curry powder
$^1/_4$ cup grated cheddar cheese

1) Preheat oven to 400°.
2) Arrange buttered hamburger buns on cooky sheet.
3) Place 1 slice pineapple on each bottom half.
4) Spread with chopped nuts and celery.
5) Place Naked Chicken breast slices over this and spread with $^1/_3$ cup mayonnaise and pinch of curry powder blended in.
6) Sprinkle with grated cheddar and bake 10 to 15 minutes until bubbly and brown.
7) Serve one bun bottom puffle and toasted, buttered top to each person.

LIFE PRESERVERS

bagels, 1 for each serving
cream cheese, softened
prosciutto, sliced paper
  thin
chopped chives
dill pickles, carrot sticks,
  ripe olives

1) Sprinkle bagels with a layer of cream cheese.
2) Spread with prosciutto and sprinkle generously with chopped chives.
3) Top with another layer of cream cheese.
4) Garnish with slivered dill pickles, carrot sticks and ripe olives.
   Servings ?????????? Let your people decide. But be sure to have lots of all ingredients on hand. This is a do-it-yourself Madwich.

LAMAJOUN

5 medium-sized rolls, halved
2 tablespoons olive oil
1½ pounds lean ground beef
½ cup chopped onion
1 tablespoon parsley, minced
½ teaspoon dried oregano
1 tablespoon chopped sweet
    pepper
1 cup shredded jack cheese
½ cup tomato sauce
¼ teaspoon sugar
    salt and pepper to taste

1) Preheat oven to 400°.
2) Scoop out dough from rolls and save for stuffing something.
3) Sauté onions in olive oil until limp, add ground beef and brown.
4) Add remaining ingredients (except for cheese) and simmer 30 minutes.
5) Scoop beef mixture evenly into the rolls. Place on cooky sheet.
6) Sprinkle each roll with shredded jack cheese.
7) Bake 10 to 15 minutes until cheese is golden and bubbly.

AVOCADWICHES
(Another do-it-yourself Madwich)

3 avocados, peeled, seeded
    and sliced
1 Spanish onion, sliced paper
    thin
3 large tomatoes, sliced
½ cup of mayonnaise blended
    with 1 teaspoon worces-
    tershire
    small bowls of wedged
    limes and crushed bird
    peppers
    salt shaker filled with de-
    hydrated Caribbean Sea
    water

1) Arrange avocados, tomatoes and onions on a bed of lettuce on a large platter.
2) Pass the mayonnaise-worcestireshire sauce, bowls of lime wedges, crushed bird peppers and the salt shaker.
3) Relax on the beach and watch the sun go down.

BAKED BEANWICHES

1 loaf of brown bread (availa-
    ble canned, if you can't
    find the fresh molasses
    type)
1 can of baked dark pea
    beans
    catsup
    butter or margarine

1) Butter slices of brown bread and spread each with about 1 tablespoon of baked beans. Put on plenty, but don't let them ooze over the edges.
2) Place on cooky sheet and bake in preheated 400° oven for about 10 minutes.
3) Dab each baked beanwich with a heaping spoonful of catsup.
   Serve with hot dogs if you're all that hungry.

CHILI SOUPWICHES

bread
mayonnaise
1 can chili soup (undiluted)
1 onion, sliced thin
    shredded cheddar cheese

1) Spread bread of your choice with mayonnaise, chili soup, then a layer of onion, and a layer of shredded cheese. Be generous.
2) Place in preheated 425° oven until cheese bubbles. Not more than 5 minutes.

PEANUT BUTTER MADWICH BIRTHDAY CAKE

  3 slices bread (thin-sliced)
for each person
      mayonnaise
      cherry tomatoes, sliced
      green onions, chopped
      peanut butter

1) Spread bread with mayonnaise.
2) Distribute tomatoes evenly over first slice.
3) Cover with second slice of bread and spread chopped green onions over this.
4) Cover with third slice of bread and spread peanut butter over top and sides.
5) Place candles on top, light them, and if no one you know is having a birthday, sing "Happy Birthday" to:
      THE MAD KING OF MADWICH!

VI

EGGBERT

Nibbles and Dips for the Queen's Picnic

It was during one of my sojourns at Buckingham Palace that I discovered Eggberts. The Queen had invited me to be the guest of honor at a picnic, and Eggberts were among the many delicacies served.

After sampling them, I begged Her Majesty's permission to visit the royal kitchens. I spoke with Oakley Wigglesworth, the *garde-manger*, who told me that Eggberts had been inspired by the following story, composed by the princess at an early age.

Once upon a time there was a little egg named Eggbert who came from a long line of royal eggs. He, his sister, Eggatha, and his brother, Eggamemnon, were offspring of a proud hen by the name of Duchess Hen Rietta. At their birth, she advised each of her chicks: "Always behave with the decorum befitting your regal ancestry. Remember, your one goal in life is to be worthy of the Queen's banquet table. *Try to keep out of trouble!*"

The three little eggs lay in their box trying to keep out of trouble until finally Eggamemnon grew restless. He pushed open the lid and rolled out and along the pantry shelf. There, below him on the stove, was a pot filled with steaming water.

"A Turkish bath!" he shouted, and dove in.

In spite of his mother's advice, Eggamemnon was in hot water. Within minutes he was a hard boiled, tough egg. Now he would never be presented at the Queen's banquet table and his career was doomed.

Eggatha next ventured forth. She climbed out of the box, meandering along the pantry shelf until she saw a bowl of strawberry jam.

"How sweet!" she cried. "Truly a befitting spot for a royal lady egg!"

She jumped in—KERPLOP!—landing with such force that she began sinking rapidly.

"Help! Help!" she shrieked. "Won't someone please get me out of this jam?"

But no one heard her.

"Blug, blug," she gasped from deep below the surface.

But still no one heard her.

And thus ended the short sweet life of Eggatha.

Following the disastrous fates that had befallen Eggatha and Eggamemnon, Duchess Hen Rietta counselled Eggbert: "Now, my son, you have always been a good egg. However, it is quite possible that you might one day be in a pretty pickle. Please do take care!"

Eggbert, who was more good than bright, interpreted this as meaning his mother wanted him to be a pretty pickle. Striving to fulfill her wishes, he left the egg box early the next morning.

"In order to become a pretty pickled egg," he reasoned, "I must first be delicately cooked."

Remembering Eggamemnon, his hard boiled, tough egg brother, he searched for, and found, a pot of cold water and rolled in. Shivering, he waited patiently until a cook came along and lit the fire beneath the pot. Then he relaxed in bliss as the water gradually warmed. The cook returned with a colander filled with brussel sprouts and was about to dump them into the pot when she saw Eggbert.

"How did you get in there, you bad little egg?" she scolded, lifting him out gently and placing him on the ledge above the stove.

Eggbert sighed with relief, for he had begun to wonder how he would ever manage to roll out of the pot. Whistling a little tune, he ambled along the ledge until he saw below him a crock filled with pickle juice—pink pickle juice. Just what he needed to be a pretty pickle!

He leapt in and within minutes he indeed was pickled. Pretty pink pickled.

Eggbert was tickled pink to be pickled pink, and his heart swelled with pride for he knew he had fulfilled his mother's highest hopes. Now he would be worthy of the Queen's banquet table.

Thanks to my persuasive charm, I managed to procure from Mr. Wigglesworth the heretofore unpublished recipe for:

PRETTY PINK PICKLED EGGBERTS

20 medium-sized eggs
1½ cups vinegar
 1 cup beet water, or juice
   from canned beets
½ box pickling spice
 2 cloves garlic
 1 tablespoon salt
   a droplet (careful!) red food
   coloring

1) Place eggs in a large saucepan with enough cold water to cover with at least an inch of water above eggs.
2) Heat water to boiling, remove pan from heat and cover tightly, letting eggs stand in hot water 15 minutes.
3) Run cold water over eggs to cool, or better still, fill sink with ice cubes and ice water. Crack shells and begin peeling eggs from large end, which contains air space.
4) Meanwhile place vinegar, beet juice, pickling spice, garlic and salt in a saucepan, add red coloring and bring to a boil, then pour over shelled hard-cooked Eggberts.
5) Place in one or two very tightly covered plastic jars and turn upside down, then rightside up, every few hours so that marinade and color covers Eggberts evenly. Leave in refrigerator at least three days, or a week. Will keep up to a month.
6) Serve whole for a picnic or, if at the Queen's banquet table, cut in half' place cut side down, and make faces: bits of ripe olive for eyes, carrot snip noses, pimiento lips. Parsley hair?*

THINK MAD

In reciprocation I presented the Queen, by way of her *garde-manger*, Mr. Wigglesworth, a number of my treasured recipes for nibbles and dips:

STUFFED CURRIED EGGBERTS

6 hard-cooked Eggberts
1/4 teaspoon salt
3/4 teaspoon dry mustard
2 teaspoons lime or lemon
    juice
1 teaspoon curry powder
1 teaspoon grated onion
1 teaspoon finely minced
    parsley
3 tablespoons mayonnaise

1) Cut hard-cooked Eggberts in half. Remove yolks and mash.
2) Add remaining ingredients and blend well, reserving whites.
3) Stuff yolk mixture into egg whites and sprinkle with paprika, dot with a caper, or decorate with a small sprig of parsley.

COCONUT STRIPPERS

1 large dry ripe coconut

1) Crack coconut and scoop out flesh.
2) Rinse nutmeat and slice wafer-thin.
3) Sprinkle with salt. Chill.

(Simple, but delightfully refreshing when the trade winds are at a lull.)

GREEN BANANA PUFFS

6 to 8 green bananas, mashed
2 tablespoons milk
2 tablespoons butter
pinch of baking powder
1 medium-sized onion,
    minced
1 egg, beaten
salt and pepper to taste
1/4 cup breadcrumbs

1) Combine bananas, milk, butter, pinch of baking powder, minced onion, and half the egg. Season.
2) Form into small balls.
3) Roll in remaining egg, then in breadcrumbs.
4) Fry in deep fat until golden brown.

BREADFRUIT BALLS

½ medium-sized breadfruit
3 tablespoons milk
1 tablespoon butter
1 onion, chopped
1 tablespoon *each* minced
    parsley and sweet pepper
1 teaspoon salt
    dash of tabasco
1 egg
¼ cup breadcrumbs

1) Peel breadfruit, place in a saucepan with water to cover and cook until tender.
2) Drain and mash. Add milk, butter, onion, parsley, sweet pepper, salt and tabasco. Blend well.
3) Form into balls and roll in egg, beaten, then in breadcrumbs.
4) Fry in deep fat until golden brown.

BOOBY BIRD'S EGGS

1) Boil eggs very gently for 5 minutes.
2) Serve at sunset with salt, freshly ground pepper and a sprinkling of lime juice.

CHIPPED BEEFIES

1 8-ounce package cream
    cheese
2 tablespoons grated onion
½ teaspoon worcestershire
3 ounces dried beef

1) Let cheese stand at room temperature until soft enough to stir smoothly. Add onion and worcestershire. Chill about 1 hour.
2) Mince dried beef very finely in a blender or with kitchen shears.
3) Form balls of the cheese mixture, marble size.
4) Roll in minced beef. Place on platter or cooky sheet and refrigerate several hours.
5) Serve on toothpicks.

PLANTAIN CHIPS

1) Slice green plantains wafer thin.
2) Fry in deep fat until golden.
3) Sprinkle with salt.

EGGPLANT DIP

2 medium-sized eggplants
1/2 cup onion, minced
1/4 cup olive oil
1/2 cup peeled tomatoes,
    chopped
1 tablespoon lime juice
salt and pepper to taste

1) Bake eggplant in preheated 350° oven until tender. About an hour.
2) Peel and chop very fine.
3) Saute onion in olive oil until golden, but not brown.
4) Add eggplant and tomato. Simmer, stirring frequently until thick. About 15 minutes.
5) Add lime juice, salt and pepper. Chill.
6) Garnish with cucumber slices and lime wedges.

SMOKED OLIVES

1 pint ripe olives (reserve all
    juice from can)
4 cloves garlic, halved
12 peppercorns
1/4 teaspoon liquid smoke
1/4 teaspoon lime or lemon
    juice

Combine all of the above. Place in jars and marinate at least two days, tightly covered.

COCONUT ROLLERS

2 3-ounce packages roquefort
    or blue cheese
4 ounces shredded cheddar
1 8-ounce package cream
    cheese
1/3 cup shredded coconut
1/2 teaspoon worcestershire

51

1) Let cheese stand at room temperature for 30 minutes or more.
2) Smash together and add worcestershire, blending thoroughly.
3) Chill for at least an hour, or overnight.
4) Shape into small balls and roll in coconut.
   Serve on toothpicks.
   About 30 balls.

CAVIAR BALLS

1 8-ounce package cream
   cheese
2 teaspoons grated onion
3 tablespoons caviar

1) Let cheese stand at room temperature until softened.
2) Place in mixing bowl and blend in grated onion and half the caviar.
3) Form into balls and roll them in remaining half of caviar until evenly coated.
4) Chill at least an hour, or overnight.
   Serve on toothpicks, with wedges of lime.
   About 20 balls.

LOBSTER LOLLAPALOOS

$^1/_4$ cup minced onion
$^1/_4$ cup mushrooms, slivered
 3 tablespoons butter or margarine
 4 eggs
$^1/_4$ cup green pepper, minced
 1 cup cream
 1 tablespoon parsley, minced
 2 tablespoons flour
 2 tablespoons sherry
   (more??)
 3 tablespoons mayonnaise
  salt to taste
 2 cups boiled crawfish or
   lobster tail, slivered

1) Sauté onion and mushrooms in butter until tender.
2) Beat eggs and mix in all remaining ingredients, except lobster, and cook until thickened, stirring constantly. Stay with it!
3) Stir in lobster.
4) Pour evenly into tart shells.

CHEESE TART SHELLS

2 cups sifted flour
3/4 teaspoon salt
1/2 cup grated Parmesan
    cheese
2/3 cup butter or margarine
5 tablespoons ice water

1) Sift flour and salt into mixing bowl. Stir in cheese.
2) Cut in butter with pastry blender or two knives.
3) Add ice water a tablespoon at a time, mixing lightly with a fork.
4) Shape pastry into a ball. Wrap in foil and refrigerate at least an hour.
5) Roll dough on a lightly floured board, then press into tartlet pans, 2½ by ½ inch. Set on cooky sheet and bake in preheated 375° oven about 10 minutes, or until golden brown.
6) Cool on wire rack 10 minutes. Then carefully remove from tartlet pans and pour in lobster.
7) At serving time, bake in preheated 375° oven about 15 minutes. Serve piping hot.
About 24 bite-size tartlets.

TURTLE LIVER PASTE

1 turtle liver (about 1
    pound)
  milk
1/2 cup mayonnaise
1/2 cup sour cream
1 teaspoon lime juice
3 crushed bird peppers or
    dash of cayenne
  salt to taste

1) Cut liver into strips and poach in just enough milk to cover.
2) When tender, remove with slotted spoon and put through meat grinder.
3) Add milk left from poaching and all remaining ingredients and mix to a smooth paste.
4) Pile into a bowl and serve with plantain chips.

TURTLE EGGS

1) Drop eggs in cold water, bring water to a boil, lower heat and simmer 10 minutes. The yolk will be hard, but the white soft, even if you double the cooking time.
2) Let cool enough to handle. Puncture an opening in each egg with a sea urchin spine. Sprinkle with salt, pepper and lime juice and squeeze into your mouth. Repeat. Repeat. Repeat. Until you run out of turtle eggs.
   At least 2 eggs for each serving.

SASSY WHELKS

2 quarts live whelks (or
  snails)
sea water

1) After capturing your whelks leave them in a bucket of sea water to de-sand themselves. Go for a swim.
2) Drain whelks and place in pot and cover with boiling salted water.
3) Cook until tender. About a half hour for a medium-sized whelk.
4) Drain and place in a large bowl, or conch shell, and provide a skewer for each participant.
5) From here on out it's a do-it-yourself whelk party. Each participant must pry out whelk with the skewer, remove brittle lid and pinch off dark end. Then dip in:

Sassy Sauce

1 tablespoon prepared mustard
1/4 cup lime juice
1 teaspoon worcestershire
1 tablespoon catsup
1/4 teaspoon tabasco, or 2
  crushed bird peppers
1 clove garlic, crunched

Mix all ingredients in a tightly covered jar and shake long and hard until thoroughly mixed.

RUMMY DOGS

1 pound small hot dogs
  (cocktail size) or Vienna
  sausages

³/₄ cup rum
1¹/₄ cup catsup
1¹/₂ cups brown sugar
1 tablespoon grated onion

1) Put hot dogs in frying pan with all other ingredients.
2) Simmer for an hour. Check now and then. If liquid dries out, splash in some more rum.
3) Pour into chafing dish.

TORTIZZAS

4 small tortillas (about 6 inches in diameter)
mozzarella cheese, sliced thin
pepperoni or salami, sliced thin
onion, minced
anchovies, minced, or anchovy paste
sweet pepper, slivered
garlic powder
oregano
basil
tomatoes, peeled and chopped

My Cousin Chris (Columbus) was the originator of this recipe for, way ahead of his time, he too was a mad thinker.

1) Place tortillas on cooky sheet and cut each into 6 sections.
2) Spread with mozzarella cheese, and top with any mad combination of the above ingredients.
3) Bake in a preheated 450° oven until bubbly. About 7 minutes.

TORTILLAS

2 cups sifted flour
¹/₂ cup water
1 teaspoon salt
¹/₄ cup shortening

1) Mix all ingredients and knead 4 dozen times on waxed paper.
2) Form into six balls and chill in a covered bowl at least half an hour.
3) Wet your hands and pat each ball into a thin round patty, about 6 inches in diameter (or use a rolling pin).
4) Fry in hot oil, one at a time, until very lightly browned.

AVOCADO DIP

1 tomato, peeled and
    chopped
2 crushed bird peppers, or a
    pinch of cayenne
1 teaspoon lime or lemon
    juice
1 onion, grated
1 tablespoon mayonnaise
  salt to taste
1 large ripe avocado

1) Combine all ingredients except avocado and let stand until ready to serve.
2) Mash avocado and mix with seasonings.
Serve with plantain chips.

CURRY DIP

1 cup mayonnaise
1/2 cup minced celery
1 teaspoon curry powder

1) Combine the above ingredients and mix thoroughly.
2) Serve dip surrounded with: celery sticks, cucumbers cut into strips, raw cauliflowerets, raw christophenes or zucchini, sliced, green onions, carrot sticks, coconut slivers.

SHRIMP REMOULADE

1 quart water
1 tablespoon salt
1 bay leaf
1 tablespoon lime or lemon
    juice
6 peppercorns
1½ pounds raw shrimp

1) In a large saucepan combine water, salt and seasonings. Bring to a boil.
2) Add shrimp. Bring to a boil again, then reduce heat and simmer, covered, 3 to 5 minutes, depending upon size of shrimp.

The Sauce

1 cup mayonnaise
1 teaspoon dry mustard

2 finely chopped hard boiled
    eggs
2 tablespoons minced parsley
1 tablespoon green pepper,
    chopped
1/2 teaspoon minced garlic
4 anchovy fillets, chopped
6 stuffed olives, finely
    chopped
1 teaspoon onion, grated
1 teaspoon lime juice
  a drop of tabasco
1 teaspoon worcestershire
    sauce
  salt and pepper to taste
    (watch out! anchovies
    and olives will do the
    salting for you.)

1) Mix well, preferably in a blender, and chill at least an hour.
2) At serving time, pile sauce into a well chilled conch shell and sink it into the center of a large bowlful of crushed ice.
3) Peel shrimp and arrange on bed of ice. Provide plenty of sea egg spines or toothpicks so guests may spear and dunk.

AVOCADO TOMATOLETS

6 slices bacon
1 basket cherry tomatoes
1 large ripe avocado
4 teaspoons lime juice
1 tablespoon finely chopped
    onion
1/4 teaspoon garlic powder
1/2 teaspoon salt
1 teaspoon chili powder
1 tablespoon mayonnaise

1) Sauté bacon until crisp. Drain, crumble and set aside.
2) Cut each cherry tomato in half lengthwise. Scoop out seed pockets and throw them into your soup pot.
3) Combine avocado, lime juice, onion, garlic, salt and chili powder. Add mayonnaise and mix well. Spoon avocado stuffing into each tomatolet half. Sprinkle with the crumbled bacon.
About 4 dozen tomatolets.

VII

BLUEBEARD'S HEEL

A *fishy tale*

On the evening of the day when Bluebeard murdered his ninth wife, Clementine, he waded into the Caribbean Sea, staring at the blood-red sunset and humming a cheery calypso tune:
"CLEMENTINE SHE BE DEAD AND GONE.
HAPPY DAYS FOR BIG DADDY FROM NOW ON!
NOW HE BE FREE TO SEARCH FOR PRETTY NEW WIFE.
MON, I TELLEEN ALL D'WORL' DIS BE D'LI————

YOOOWEEEEEEE*********UUUUUUUUUUUUUUUU UU!!!!!!!!!!*****§§§§§!!!"
The pirate let forth an earsplitting shriek, for he had trod upon a spiny sea egg. Still screaming with pain and emitting profanities, he hobbled back to shore to nurse his wounded heel.

The moral of this story is obvious to anyone with a philosophic turn of mind. Namely:

```
*******************************
*                             *
* TIME WOUNDS ALL HEELS *
*******************************
```

SEA EGGS

4 sea eggs
1/8 cup lime juice
1/8 cup sea water

1) Spear sea eggs with long sharp-pointed stick.
2) Place in an old basket and shake hard, to remove as many spines as possible.

3) Wade in to shore and, turning large opening of sea eggs toward you, split each in half with a fishing knife.
4) Remove and discard grinder, scoop out fillets and rinse them in sea water.
5) Arrange cleaned fillets on a tray covered with sea grape leaves.
6) Spear raw fillets with skewers, or improvised dipping sticks, and dunk in lime juice-sea water mixture.
7) Savor on the beach, at sunset.
   4 servings.

FISH AND FUNGI

2 cups onions, sliced thin
2 cups tomatoes, peeled
4 tablespoons vegetable oil
1 tablespoon chopped par-
   sley
1 teaspoon lime juice
1 pound fish fillets
salt and pepper to taste

1) Sauté onions in oil, until yellow.
2) Add tomatoes, parsley, lime juice, and salt and pepper to taste.
3) Simmer until sauce thickens.
4) Add fish fillets and cook for 10 minutes.

FUNGI

1¹/₂ cups cornmeal
1 quart and 1 cup water
1 teaspoon salt
¹/₂ cup okra, sliced in half
   inch pieces
2 tablespoons butter or margarine
¹/₄ teaspoon freshly ground
   black pepper

1) Bring one quart water to a boil. Add salt.
2) Mix cornmeal with remaining cup of cold water and add to boiling water a little at a time, stirring constantly until thickened. About 15 minutes.
3) Add okra, butter and pepper.
4) Pour into a greased baking dish and chill until ready to use.

5) Slice fungi and alternate with fish fillets in baking dish. Cover with the sauce and reheat in oven for 20 minutes at 350°.

4 to 6 servings.

RAY

corn meal
salt and pepper
wings of ray sliced into
   long thin strips (quanti-
   ties depend upon size of
   ray)
lime juice
cooking oil

1) Mix cornmeal, salt and pepper and dip each strip in lime juice and then cornmeal mixture, coating on all sides.
2) Heat oil in heavy frying pan and sauté strips until golden.
3) Serve with lime wedges.

WHELKS AND RICE

4 dozen or more whelks (substitute snails, if you can't
   find any whelks)
sea water

1) Keep whelks in sea water until ready to use. Drain.
2) Boil in salted water to cover until easily removed from shell with a nut pick. Cut into small pieces.
3) Simmer over very low heat for 2 to 3 hours in the following sauce:

WHELK SAUCE

6 cloves garlic, very finely
   minced
1/4 cup olive oil
3 onions, chopped
6 tomatoes, peeled
2 cans tomato paste and one
   can water
2 teaspoons salt
1 tablespoon sugar
1/2 teaspoon oregano
3 drops tabasco
1/4 teaspoon freshly ground
   black pepper
1 bay leaf

1) Simmer garlic in olive oil in a heavy skillet over lowest possible heat. Watch it. Don't let it brown.
2) When garlic is tender add remaining ingredients and whelks. Remove bay leaf after first half hour.
3) Serve over steamed rice.
   4 to 6 servings?? Well now. How many whelks did you capture? And if you have neither whelks nor snails in your possession, make the sauce anyway and serve over spaghetti.

DEVILED WHELKS

1 cup cooked whelks, ground
$^1/_2$ cup breadcrumbs
1 medium onion, minced
1 tablespoon mayonnaise
1 tablespoon butter
3 drops tabasco sauce
1 teaspoon minced parsley
1 teaspoon lime juice
2 eggs, lightly beaten
$^1/_2$ cup hot water

1) Combine all ingredients and mix well.
2) Distribute evenly in 6 ramekins or scallop shells. Sprinkle with toasted buttered breadcrumbs and bake at 350° until brown.
   6 servings.

WHELK CHOWDER

4 dozen whelks, cooked and
    ground
2 strips bacon, cut into small
    bits
3 large onions, chopped
6 medium potatoes, diced
2 tablespoons flour
salt and pepper
monosodium glutamate
1 quart milk
$^1/_2$ cup whelk broth
chopped parsley

1) Pinch soft tails from whelks and put firm white muscle through meat grinder, or chop very fine.
2) Sauté bacon; add onions and potatoes and cook until golden.

3) Transfer above to a heavy kettle, add enough water to cover, and simmer until potatoes are tender.
4) Sprinkle with flour very slowly, stirring constantly. Watch out for lumps!
5) Add whelks, then salt, pepper and monosodium glutamate to taste.
6) Combine milk and whelk broth and heat, but do not boil. Add gradually to above mixture, stirring madly until chowder is smooth and creamy.
7) Serve in preheated bowls and sprinkle with chopped parsley.
   4 to 6 hearty servings.

CONCH

**6 conchs in shell (yield about
   1 pound)**

1) Cover conchs with boiling salted water and cook until meat curls and can easily be removed from shell. This method keeps the pink shell intact.

OR

2) The more popular West Indian way is to break off the lower tip of the shell, draw out the flesh, and boil. The shell may then be used as a horn, which is a recognized distress signal.

   In Frenchtown, St. Thomas, when a fisherman has a good catch, he blows his conch horn to let everyone within earshot know he has fish for sale.

CONCH CHOWDER

**1 pound conch meat, pre-
   pared as above
¹/₄ cup lime juice
2 onions, diced
3 cloves garlic, finely minced
¹/₂ cup chopped celery
2 cans tomato paste
1 quart water
4 potatoes, diced
1 teaspoon salt
2 crushed bird peppers or a
   pinch of cayenne
¹/₂ cup chopped parsley
¹/₄ cup oil**

1) Put conch through meat grinder, or pound with edge of a plate or mallet until meat is in pieces, then dice with a knife.
2) Pour lime juice over meat and let stand several hours or overnight.
3) Sauté onion, garlic and celery in oil until tender, but not brown.
4) Add tomato paste and simmer 10 minutes.
5) Add water, salt and pepper and bring to a boil. Add potatoes and simmer 10 minutes.
6) Add conch meat and continue simmering until potatoes are tender, but not falling apart.
7) At serving time, top each bowlful with chopped parsley.
6 servings.

PEPPERED CONCH AND RICE

2 tablespoons flour
2 tablespoons butter
2 cups cream
1/2 can cream of mushroom
    soup
2 cups cooked conch, cut into
    bite size pieces
    juice of 1 lime
4 bird peppers, crushed, or
    cayenne to taste
1 tablespoon green onions,
    chopped
1 tablespoon parsley,
    chopped
    monosodium glutamate and
    salt to taste

1) Blend flour and butter in top of double boiler and add cream very gradually, stirring constantly.
2) Gradually add undiluted cream of mushroom soup and continue stirring.
3) Add remaining ingredients.
4) Serve over rice.
4 to 6 servings.

TURTLE STEW

1/4 cup lime juice
1 1/2 pounds turtle meat, cubed
2 large onions, chopped

63

2 cloves garlic, finely minced
1 sweet pepper, chopped
1/4 cup oil
1 cup tomatoes, peeled and
    chopped
  salt and pepper to taste
6 medium-sized potatoes
1 cup sherry

1) Pour lime juice over meat and let stand at least two hours, or overnight, refrigerated.
2) Sauté onions, garlic and sweet pepper in oil until tender.
3) Add all of remaining ingredients, except potatoes, and simmer until gravy thickens and meat is tender. About 30 minutes, but timing depends upon size of your turtle: the larger, the tougher.
4) Add potatoes and continue simmering until they are tender.

OR

Forget the potatoes and serve over rice.
5) At serving time, sprinkle a teaspoon of sherry over each bowl.

6 servings.

LITTLE THATCH SEAFOOD BAKE

1 cup dry egg noodles
1 10 1/2-ounce can mushroom
    soup
1/2 cup mayonnaise
1/2 cup sweet pepper, chopped
1/2 cup onion, chopped
1/2 cup celery, chopped
1 teaspoon worcestershire
1 teaspoon lime or lemon
    juice
1 cup breadcrumbs, buttered
1 cup cooked, shelled
    shrimp, deveined, or 1
    4 1/2-ounce can of shrimp,
    drained
2 cups cooked crabmeat,
    flaked, or 7 1/2-ounce can
    crabmeat, drained
1 teaspoon grated fresh gin-
    ger root or 1/4 teaspoon
    ginger powder
  a whisper of garlic powder
  a splash of dry Vermouth
  salt and pepper to taste

1) Cook egg noodles and drain. *Do not overcook.*
2) Combine with all remaining ingredients except buttered crumbs, and mix well.
3) Place in a 2½ quart casserole and top with buttered crumbs.
4) Bake in preheated 350° oven for 30 minutes.
   4 to 6 servings.

COQUILLE GRANDPÈRE ANTOINE

2 pounds scallops
2 cups dry white wine
½ teaspoon salt
½ teaspoon monosodium glu-
    tamate
  herb bouquet
½ pound mushrooms, sliced
½ cup onion, minced
1 tablespoon parsley, minced
3 tablespoons butter
3 tablespoons lime juice and
    water
¼ cup butter
¼ cup flour
2 egg yolks
¼ cup mayonnaise
  breadcrumbs

1) Rinse scallops in cold water and drain on paper towels.
2) Heat white wine and add scallops, salt and monosodium glutamate. Add herb bouquet.
3) Simmer about 10 minutes, or until tender. Remove herbs.
4) Drain scallops and cut into chunks. Set aside. Reserve juice.
5) Simmer mushrooms with minced onion and parsley in 3 tablespoons butter. Add 3 tablespoons water and lime juice.
6) Combine ¼ cup butter and ¼ cup flour in a double boiler and gradually stir in reserved liquid, then egg yolks and mayonnaise.
7) Combine all of the above and distribute evenly in scallop shells, or ramekins. Sprinkle with breadcrumbs and dot with butter.
8) Bake in a preheated 450° oven for 8 to 10 minutes, until crumbs are browned.
   6 to 8 servings.

LANGOUSTE FLAMBE

3 tablespoons olive oil
$\frac{1}{2}$ cup lime juice
$\frac{1}{2}$ cup catsup
1 teaspoon black pepper
3 crawfish or lobster tails,
    boiled and split in half
$\frac{1}{2}$ cup 100 proof rum, heated

1) Warm olive oil, lime juice, catsup and pepper in saucepan.
2) Remove lobster from shells and cut into large chunks, carefully reserving shells.
3) Add crawfish or lobster tail meat to sauce and cook over low heat 5 minutes.
4) Fill shells with mixture.
5) Place half lobster on each plate and pour heated rum over it. Set aflame just before serving.
   6 flamboyant servings. So why not dine in the shade of your flamboyant tree?

LONGOUSTE STU-FU

3 crawfish or lobster tails,
    boiled and split in half
1 large onion, chopped
$\frac{1}{4}$ pound mushrooms,
    chopped
4 tablespoons butter, plus a
    few dabs for topping
1 tablespoon flour
$\frac{1}{2}$ cup Naked Chicken Stock
    (page 91)
1 tablespoon mayonnaise
3 drops tabasco
    juice of 1 lime
    whisper of tarragon
3 tablespoons sherry
    salt to taste
$\frac{1}{2}$ cup breadcrumbs
$\frac{1}{2}$ cup grated parmesan
    cheese

1) Remove meat from boiled lobsters and cut into small chunks. Reserve shells and set aside.
2) Sauté onion and mushrooms in 3 tablespoons butter until tender. Slowly add flour, mixing well.
3) Add stock, mayonnaise, tabasco, lime juice and tarragon.

4) When mixture has thickened, add lobster, sherry and salt to taste. Place in shells.
5) Combine breadcrumbs with parmesan cheese and remaining tablespoon of butter and sprinkle over lobster. Dot with butter.
6) Bake in preheated 350° oven 15 minutes, or until golden brown.
7) Garnish with lime wedges.
   6 servings.

STUFFED LAND CRABS

12 land crabs
 6 green onions, chopped
 1 sweet pepper, chopped
 1 teaspoon parsley, minced
 1 teaspoon fresh thyme,
     minced, or 1/4 teaspoon
     dried thyme
   salt and pepper to taste
 1 teaspoon lime juice
 1 tablespoon worcestershire
   dried breadcrumbs
1/4 cup butter

1) Plunge live crabs in cold, salted water to cover and bring slowly to a boil, then simmer 15 minutes.
2) Pick out the meat with a nut pick and mix with sauteed onion, sweet pepper, parsley, thyme, and salt and pepper to taste. Add lime juice, worcestershire, and most of the breadcrumbs, reserving enough to sprinkle over crab-meat.
3) Clean crab shells and place crab mixture in them. Sprinkle with dried breadcrumbs and dot with butter.
4) Brown in preheated 450° oven.

CRAB LOAFER

   1 cup milk
   4 tablespoons melted butter
1 1/2 cups soft breadcrumbs
   2 cups flaked cooked crab-
       meat
   3 egg yolks, lightly beaten
   2 tablespoons lime juice
   2 tablespoons minced onion
 1/2 cup minced celery

67

^{1}/$_2$ teaspoon salt
^{1}/$_4$ teaspoon pepper
3 egg whites, beaten stiff

1) Scald milk and place in mixing bowl. Add breadcrumbs and melted butter. Blend until smooth.
2) Combine with crabmeat and remaining ingredients, reserving egg whites until last. Gently fold them in.
3) Grease a loaf pan and spread crab mixture in it.
4) Bake in a preheated 350° oven for 35 minutes.
5) Serve hot, garnished with lime and tomato wedges.
   6 servings.

TUNA TUMBLE

1 8-ounce package of noodles
^{1}/$_2$ cup onion, chopped
^{1}/$_2$ cup celery, finely chopped
^{1}/$_2$ cup green pepper, finely
   chopped
^{1}/$_4$ cup butter
^{1}/$_4$ cup flour
^{1}/$_2$ teaspoon dry mustard
1 teaspoon salt
3 drops tabasco
^{1}/$_2$ teaspoon black pepper
2 cups milk
2 cups bonita, cooked and
   flaked, or a 7^1/$_2$-ounce
   can of tuna, drained
2 cups small curd cottage
   cheese
1 tablespoon lime or lemon
   juice
^{1}/$_2$ cup buttered breadcrumbs

1) Cook noodles according to package directions.
2) Sauté onion, celery and green pepper in butter until tender.
3) Blend in flour and seasonings.
4) Add milk and stir constantly until mixture thickens.
5) Combine with drained noodles, bonita, cottage cheese, and lime juice.
6) Pour into a greased 2 quart casserole and sprinkle with buttered crumbs.
7) Bake in preheated 350° oven 30 to 40 minutes.
   6 servings.
   (May be prepared well in advance and refrigerated. If so, add 15 minutes to baking time.

SHRIMP YO HO HO!

2 pounds medium-sized
    shrimp (26 to 30)
1/8 teaspoon salt
1/4 cup vegetable oil
1/4 teaspoon powdered ginger
    or
1/2 teaspoon ginger root, grat-
    ed
1/4 teaspoon garlic powder
1/4 cup light rum
2 teaspoons cornstarch dis-
    solved in 1/2 cup water
2 tablespoons soy sauce
6 green onions, cut into 1 1/2
    inch lengths

1) Peel and devein cleaned shrimp and dry with paper towels.
2) Heat wok or skillet; add oil and salt.
3) Turn heat to medium and add shrimp. Sprinkle with ginger and garlic powder. Add rum and cook 4 minutes.
4) Add dissolved cornstarch, soy sauce and green onions, stirring constantly until sauce thickens. Not more than 2 minutes.
Serve with rice.
4 servings.

SAPPHIRE BAY SCRAMBLE

2 pounds fresh albacore or
    red snapper
    juice of 1 lime
    salt to taste
1 onion, minced
1 cup coconut milk
1 tomato, peeled and
    chopped
1 sweet pepper, chopped
1 hard boiled egg, chopped
1 cucumber, chopped
1/4 cup shredded coconut

1) Slice raw fish paper-thin. Sprinkle with lime juice, add salt and chill at least 2 hours, stirring now and then.
2) Add onion, coconut milk and half each of remaining ingredients. Blend and chill.

3) Combine fish mixture with coconut blend, place in chilled serving dish and garnish with remainder of chopped tomato, sweet pepper, hard boiled egg, cucumber and shredded coconut.
4) Serve cold on Sapphire Beach on a balmy August night. 8 appetizer or 4 main course servings.

COCONUT MILK

1) Pare brown skin from coconut meat and blend with 1 cup scalded milk. Let stand 20 minutes, then strain, and shred meat.

OR

2) 1 cup packaged shredded coconut may be substituted for fresh coconut.

SOUSED GRUNT or GRO-GRO

4 fresh grunts
  blade of mace, or a pinch
    of powdered mace
1 bay leaf
3 whole cloves
1/4 cup lime juice
2 crushed bird peppers or a
    pinch of cayenne

1) Wash and fillet grunts and sprinkle each with remaining ingredients.
2) Place in a casserole and bake for about 1 hour in a preheated 325° oven.
3) Cool. Refrigerate and serve well chilled.

BAKED STUFFED GROUPER

1 6-to-8 pound grouper
1 lime, halved
1 teaspoon *each*: salt, pepper,
    fresh thyme and parsley
1 onion, chopped fine
4 strips bacon

1) Rub inside cavity of grouper with lime and seasonings, reserving bacon.
2) Stuff fish and fasten together with skewers.

3) Place in baking pan, layer bacon strips over fish and cover with foil. Allow 12 to 15 minutes per pound in a preheated 350° oven. Reduce heat to 300° after the first 30 minutes.
4) Remove foil for the last 15 minutes. Serve with the following sauce:

GROUPER SAUCE

3 thinly sliced onions
1 cup fish broth or stock
1/4 cup lime juice
1/4 cup butter
    salt and pepper to taste

1) Simmer onions in fish stock until tender.
2) Place in double boiler and stir in remaining ingredients.

THE STUFFING

2 cups breadcrumbs
4 hard boiled eggs, chopped
1/2 cup onion, finely chopped
4 tablespoons butter or mar-
    garine
1 tablespoon *each*: capers
    and parsley

ALEWIFE CHOWDER

1 4-pound alewife, or other
    white fleshed fish such as
    parrot, porgy or cod,
    which should yield 2
    pounds boneless meat
2 large onions, thinly sliced
1 tablespoon butter or mar-
    garine
4 potatoes, thinly sliced
    salt and pepper to taste
1 cup fish stock
1 cup cream
    chopped parsley

1) Cover head and bones of the poor departed alewife with water and simmer.
2) Sauté onions in butter in a heavy kettle until yellow (the onions, not the kettle).
3) Add potatoes, salt, pepper and boned fish, and steam about 10 minutes.

4) Strain fish broth from head and bones of alewife and add 1 cup to above mixture. Simmer for about 1 hour.
5) Heat cream and add to chowder just before serving.
6) Serve in heated soup bowls and sprinkle with chopped parsley.
6 to 8 servings.

GINGER FISH FILLETS

3 tablespoons olive oil
3 tablespoons butter or mar-
    garine
6 fish fillets
2 cloves garlic, very finely
    minced
1/2 teaspoon powdered ginger
    or 1 tablespoon shredded
    fresh ginger root
1 tablespoon sugar
1 tablespoon lime juice
2 tablespoons soy sauce
1 tablespoon cornstarch dis-
    solved in 1/4 cup water
6 tablespoons water
3 green onions, cut in 1 1/2
    inch slices

1) Heat olive oil and butter in a heavy frying pan or wok. Cook fish fillets 3 or 4 minutes or more, depending on thickness of fillets, turning frequently.
2) Transfer fish to warm platter, add garlic and ginger to oil remaining in skillet. Stir like a maniac to be sure not to let garlic brown.
3) Mix sugar with lime juice and soy sauce and add.
4) Combine cornstarch and water and gradually stir into mixture in the skillet. Keep stirring until sauce is smooth and thickened.
5) Pour sauce over the fish. Sprinkle with green onions and serve.
6 servings.

BAKED BARRACUDA STEAKS
(Substitute kingfish or any other firm-fleshed fish steaks)

2 onions, sliced thin
1 clove garlic, minced
1/2 tablespoon butter or mar-
    garine

1 tablespoon olive oil
$1/4$ cup parsley, minced
$1/2$ teaspoon salt
$1/8$ teaspoon pepper
$1/2$ cup tomatoes, peeled and
    chopped
1 tablespoon tomato paste
$1/4$ cup Naked Chicken stock
    (page 90)
1 tablespoon white wine
$1/2$ teaspoon sugar
4 fish steaks
4 tomato slices, unpeeled
4 lime slices

1) Sauté onion and garlic until tender, but not brown.
2) Add remaining ingredients, except fish steaks, and simmer 30 minutes. So much for the sauce. Now:

4 barracuda steaks
4 tomato slices, unpeeled
4 lime slices

1) Place fish steaks in greased baking dish and cover with the sauce.
2) Top each with a tomato slice; then top tomato slice with lime slice.
3) Pour on the sauce and bake in preheated 350° oven for about 20 minutes (timing will vary with thickness of steaks).
   4 servings.

VIII

GERTRUDE, NUDE PRUDE

A fowl at play?

CONCEITED YOUNG CHICKEN, SHE NAME
    BE GERTRUDE
HAVE D'REPUTATION FOR BE-EEN A PRUDE
'TIL ONE DAY TO SHOW OFF SHE PULCHRITUDE
SHE SHED ALL SHE FEATHERS AN' PARADE
    AROUND NUDE,
DEN FALL IN HOT WATAH AN' GET SHESELF
    STEWED,
AN' DAT BE D'SAD END OF POOR GERTRUDE.

So goes the calypso verse that brought immortality to Gertrude shortly after her demise at the turn of the century. But the song in no way reveals the complexity of the incident. My neighbor, Pierre Le Duc, and I, are among the few surviving St. Thomians who recall it. The following is the gist of what occurred.

The allegedly prudish chicken, Gertrude, was the treasured possession of Pierre's cousin, Emile, who lives on Frenchman's Hill on the Atlantic side of the island. One morning she disappeared mysteriously, and the distraught Emile roamed St. Thomas searching for her. His last stop was Frenchtown, and when he entered Pierre Le Duc's home, through unfortunate coincidence (???) the aroma of steamed chicken assaulted his nostrils.

"Oh, my Gertrude," Emile moaned, rushing to the stove. He gazed into the pot and sobbed bitterly.

Pierre sputtered his denial, but to no avail. That afternoon Emile filed suit, and after a prolonged trial that ended in a hung jury, the case was dismissed.

74

The unresolved question was, and to this day remains:

Was Gertrude merely a capricious addle-brained frivolous wanton—in short, a playful fowl?

Or was she the victim of fowl play?

Whatever the answer, although Gertrude was vain, she did not die in vain. For it was she who inspired my renowned recipe:

NAKED CHICKEN

Take one conceited young playful chicken (a 2 to 2¹/₂ pound broiler-fryer).

Add:
- **2 green onions, quartered**
- **3 slices of ginger**
- **2 teaspoons salt**
- **1 teaspoon monosodium glutamate**
- **soy sauce**

1) Boil 3 pints of water in a heavy pot.
2) Add chicken, onion, ginger, and salt.
3) Boil 7 minutes, breast down. Turn breast up and boil 7 minutes more.
4) Remove from fire and set aside to cool, keeping pot tightly covered. *Do not raise lid.* Have a dip in the sea for an hour or three.
5) When trade winds are low, serve Gertrude, chilled, with soy sauce. Or reheat and serve with steamed rice.
   4 to 6 servings.

DRUNKY CHICKEN

- **3 2-pound broiler-fryers, quartered**
- **2 green peppers, chopped**
- **4 peeled tomatoes, chopped**
- **3 onions, chopped**
- **2 cloves garlic, minced**
- **1 teaspoon salt**
- **1 teaspoon freshly ground pepper**
- **1 teaspoon monosodium glutamate**
- **1 teaspoon sugar**
- **1 teaspoon fresh oregano or ¹/₂ teaspoon dried**

2 tablespoons chopped parsley
1/2 cup red wine
1/4 cup lime juice
1/2 cup olive oil
2 tablespoons tomato paste
1/4 cup sliced stuffed green
  olives

1) Place chicken in bowl and add green peppers, tomatoes, onions, garlic, salt, pepper, monosodium glutamate, sugar, oregano, parsley, wine and lime juice.
2) Cover and marinate for at least three hours, or overnight, refrigerated.
3) Remove chicken from marinade, reserving liquid.
4) Heat olive oil in large skillet. Brown chicken on all sides.
5) Add reserved marinade, tomato paste and olives.
6) Cook over low heat, covered, for an hour, or until chicken is tender.
   6 servings.

GRANDPÈRE ANTOINE'S CREOLE

2 2-to-2 1/2 pound fryers, disjointed
1/4 cup olive oil
1 1-pound 12 ounce can tomatoes
2 tablespoons butter
1 teaspoon salt
1/4 teaspoon pepper
1 teaspoon chopped fresh
  thyme, or 1/4 teaspoon
  dried
1 tablespoon minced parsley
1 bay leaf
3 cloves garlic, minced
1 tablespoon flour
1/2 cup minced onion
1/2 cup chopped green pepper
1/2 cup white wine

1) Brown chicken in olive oil.
2) Combine tomatoes and one tablespoon butter and simmer for 10 minutes, stirring occasionally.
3) Add salt, pepper, thyme, parsley, bay leaf and garlic, and cook about half an hour, until sauce thickens.
4) Melt one tablespoon butter, blend in flour, and cook until brown.

5) Add onion and green pepper, and brown slightly.
6) Add wine, stirring constantly, until sauce thickens.
7) Add chicken and tomato sauce. Cover and simmer 45 minutes, or until chicken is tender.
4 to 6 servings.

CHICKEN AUNTY PASTO

2 2-to-2½ pound broiler-
    fryers, quartered
¼ pound butter or margarine
2 tablespoons olive oil
4 medium-sized carrots
3 onions
2 ½ inch slices salami, cut in
    1 inch cubes
1 (1-pound, 12-ounce) can
    peas
½ cup red wine
    salt and pepper to taste

1) Rub chicken with butter or margarine and 1 tablespoon olive oil.
2) Sprinkle with salt and freshly ground pepper.
3) Place chicken skin side down on a greased deep baking dish.
4) Place uncovered in preheated oven at 350° and bake 25 minutes.
5) Turn chicken once, and if too dry brush with olive oil.
6) Return to oven and bake 15 minutes longer.
7) Meanwhile grate carrots and onions coarsely. Set aside.
8) Heat 1 tablespoon of olive oil in a saucepan. Add salami and saute for one minute. Add grated carrots, onions and peas with liquid.
9) Cook over medium fire 8 minutes, stirring occasionally.
10) Pour over chicken and add wine. Bake 15 to 20 minutes longer, or until tender.
Serves 4 to 6.

POLLO DEL SOL

1 3-to-3½ pound broiler-fryer
    salt and pepper
    monosodium glutamate
1 6-ounce can frozen concen-
    trated orange juice
2 orange juice cans of water
¼ cup butter or margarine

3 medium onions, sliced thin
1 teaspoon lime or lemon
   juice

1) Place chicken in baking pan and sprinkle with salt, pepper and monosodium glutamate.
2) Heat orange juice, water, butter, onions and lime juice to blend.
3) Pour over chicken.
4) Bake in preheated 350° oven for 1½ to 2 hours.
   Serves 4 to 6.

SWEET 'N' SMOKY

½ cup catsup
2 tablespoons prepared mustard
½ cup vegetable oil
¼ cup vinegar
½ cup maple syrup
1 3-to-3½ pound broiler-
   fryer, disjointed
½ cup water
1 large onion, sliced
1 teaspoon hickory smoked
   salt
¼ teaspoon pepper

1) Combine catsup, mustard, oil, vinegar and maple syrup.
2) Place chicken fat side up in a baking pan.
3) Pour ½ cup water in bottom of pan and tuck onion slices around chicken.
4) Sprinkle with hickory smoked salt and pepper.
5) Place in preheated 375° oven and bake for 30 minutes.
6) Remove from oven and pour barbecue sauce (Step 1) over chicken.
7) Return to oven and bake 30 minutes longer, basting every 10 minutes.
   Serves 4 to 6.

EGGPLANT STUFFED CHICKEN

1½ cup diced eggplant, peeled
   and cubed
¼ cup grated parmesan
   cheese

¼ cup parsley, minced
1 cup toasted breadcrumbs
¼ teaspoon pepper
¼ teaspoon dried oregano
¼ cup butter or margarine
1 3-to-3½ pound broiler-fryer
1 tablespoon olive oil
1 tablespoon sherry
   salt, pepper and monoso-
     dium glutamate

1) Preheat oven to 350°.
2) Combine eggplant with next six ingredients.
3) Rub chicken with half of the olive oil and sherry, salt, pepper and monosodium glutamate.
4) Lightly fill neck and body cavities with eggplant stuffing. Do not pack in.
5) Bake for about an hour and a half, or until tender.
6) Place leftover stuffing in shallow dish and bake during last half hour.
   4 to 6 servings.

BLUSHING CHICKEN

¼ pound butter or margarine
2 2-to-2½ pound broiler-
   fryers, quartered
1 large onion, sliced thin
½ cup sherry
½ cup tomato juice
1 tablespoon paprika
   salt, pepper and monoso-
     dium glutamate
1 cup water

1) Melt butter. Add chicken and braise until light brown.
2) Remove and place in broiling pan.
3) Sauté onion in butter left in pan. Add other ingredients and 1 cup water, and pour over chicken.
4) Bake in preheated 400° oven, uncovered.
5) Turn after half an hour.
6) Cook another half hour.
7) Turn again and cook 15 minutes.
   6 to 8 servings.

CHICKEN CRUNCH AND MUNCH

2 cups cooked chicken (1 3-
    pound broiler-fryer),
    boned
2 cups chopped celery
1/3 cup green pepper, chopped
3 tablespoons pimiento,
    sliced
2 tablespoons grated onion
2 tablespoons lime juice
1 teaspoon parsley, minced
1 teaspoon salt
1/2 cup slivered almonds
1 cup mayonnaise
1/2 cup grated cheese
1 1/2 cups crumbled french fried
    onion rings

1) Butter a 7 by 11 inch pan.
2) Combine all of the above ingredients except cheese and
    crumbled onion rings and pour into pan.
3 Sprinkle with the cheese, then top with onions.
4 Bake at 350° in preheated oven about 30 minutes.
    4 to 6 servings.

PIRATE'S LOOT

2 2-to-2 1/2 pound broiler-
    fryers
1/4 cup olive oil
2 medium onions, chopped
2 cloves garlic, minced
2/3 cup peeled tomatoes,
    chopped
1 1/2 quarts chicken broth
1 bay leaf
1 pound rice
    generous pinch of saffron
1/4 cup green pepper, chopped
    salt to taste

1) Sauté chicken in olive oil. Add onions and garlic, then
    remaining ingredients. Stir thoroughly.
2) Bake in preheated 350° oven 20 to 30 minutes, or until
    chicken is tender.

NUTTY CHICKEN

1 pound cubed, boned, raw
  chicken or turkey
3/4 teaspoon salt
2 tablespoons cornstarch
3 tablespoons soy sauce
2 tablespoons sherry
1 tablespoon sugar
3 tablespoons vegetable oil
1 cup chopped celery
1 cup chopped onion
8 water chestnuts, cubed
1 cup bamboo shoots, cubed
1/4 cup Naked Chicken stock°
1/2 pound chopped walnuts

1) Dredge chicken or turkey in mixture of salt, cornstarch, soy sauce, sherry and sugar.
2) Heat pan (preferably a wok) and add oil. Sauté dredged chicken until tender; drain on paper towels.
3) Combine celery, onion, water chestnuts and bamboo shoots and sauté about 5 minutes in remaining oil. Remove from pan.
4) Reheat pan and add chicken and chicken stock and heat thoroughly. Add sautéed vegetables and walnut meats. *Do not overcook.*
5) Serve on a bed of rice.
  4 to 6 servings.
  ° See page 91

GARBANZAROO

2 teaspoons salt or a pinch
  more, to taste
1/2 teaspoon pepper
1/4 cup flour
2 3-pound chickens, disjointed
1/3 cup olive oil
1 cup canned garbanzos,
  drained
3 onions, quartered
2 tomatoes, peeled and
  chopped
2 green peppers, sliced
1 1/2 cups red wine
1/4 teaspoon ground chili pepper

¹/₄ teaspoon oregano, dried
1 bay leaf

1) Combine salt, pepper and flour. Roll chicken parts in it lightly.
2) Heat olive oil in heavy saucepan. Add chicken and brown well. Add garbanzos, onions, tomatoes, green pepper, wine, chili peppers, oregano and bay leaf.
3) Cover and cook over low heat for 1 hour, or until chicken is tender. Remove bay leaf.
6 to 8 servings.

CHICKEN DASHEEN

4 cups cooked, coarsely
    chopped, dasheen greens
    or spinach
1 cup sharp cheddar cheese,
    shredded
4 chicken breasts, boned and
    sliced

1) Place dasheen greens in four individual buttered casseroles.
2) Sprinkle with half the cheese.
3) Place slices of chicken breast on dasheen greens and sprinkle with more cheese, reserving some for topping.
4) Cover with the following sauce:

¹/₄ cup butter or margarine
¹/₂ cup flour
1 teaspoon salt
¹/₈ teaspoon pepper
1 cup milk
4 tablespoons mayonnaise
¹/₂ teaspoon nutmeg
3 tablespoons sherry
1 tablespoon worcestershire

1) Slowly heat butter until melted, and remove from heat.
2) Add flour, salt and pepper, stirring until smooth.
3) Add milk, a small amount at a time, stirring after each addition. Return to heat.
4) Over medium heat, bring to a boil, stirring constantly. Reduce heat and simmer 1 minute.
5) Gradually add mayonnaise, nutmeg, sherry and worcestershire. Pour over chicken and sprinkle with remaining cheese.
6) Bake in preheated 450° oven until golden brown.
4 lavish servings.

COKI BAY CORMA

1 3½-pound broiler-fryer,
   disjointed
½ cup yogurt
1 teaspoon fresh ginger root,
   grated, or ¼ teaspoon
   powdered
¾ teaspoon salt
1 tablespoon curry powder
2 teaspoons garlic, finely
   minced
2 teaspoons butter or margarine
1 cup onions, chopped
1 cup Naked Chicken stock*
2 teaspoons slivered almonds

1) Place chicken in mixing bowl.
2) Combine yogurt with the ginger, salt, curry powder and
   half the garlic, and pour over chicken.
3) Marinate at room temperature for two hours, basting
   frequently.
4) Melt butter in a heavy saucepan and saute onions and
   remaining garlic over low heat about five minutes,
   stirring frequently. Push to one side. Add chicken and
   sauté until golden, then add chicken stock. Cover and
   simmer over a low heat for 30 to 45 minutes, or until
   tender.
5) Add almonds five minutes before serving.
   4 to 6 servings. With rice, of course.

* See page 91

MATILDA! (She's a honey.)

¼ cup butter
1 teaspoon curry powder
1 teaspoon grated fresh ginger, or ¼ teaspoon powdered ginger
1 teaspoon salt
1 2½ to 3 pound broiler-
   fryer, disjointed
½ cup honey
1 tablespoon prepared mustard

1) Melt butter and add dry ingredients.
2) Dredge chicken in the above. Add honey and mustard, rubbing whole mixture over chicken parts.
3) Place skin side down and bake in preheated 375° oven for half an hour.
4) Turn to other side and continue baking for another hour, basting every 10 minutes.

PEANUT BUTTER STEW

1 3 pound broiler-fryer, disjointed
1 teaspoon seasoned salt
2 tablespoons vegetable oil
2 or more cups water
1 cup tomatoes, peeled and
   chopped
1/4 cup tomato paste
1 large onion, chopped
3 crushed bird peppers, or a
   pinch of cayenne pepper
salt to taste
1/2 cup peanut butter

1) Sprinkle chicken with seasoned salt. Sear in oil in a heavy skillet, turning frequently until chicken is golden brown. Cover with one cup of water and simmer for 10 minutes.
2) Add all other ingredients, except the remaining cup of water and peanut butter, and simmer 20 minutes.
3) Bring remaining cup of water to a boil and very gradually add the peanut butter, stirring madly until mixture is smooth. Pour over chicken and simmer 10 minutes longer, or until chicken is tender. Add more water if needed.

6 to 8 servings. Serve with rice or noodles.

CHICKEN IN COCONUT SHELL

1 medium-sized coconut
1/2 cup chicken stock
1/4 cup coconut milk
1 tablespoon dry Vermouth
1 teaspoon soy sauce
1/4 teaspoon curry powder
2 tablespoons cornstarch
1 cup Naked Chicken,*
   boned and sliced
1 tablespoon grated coconut

1) Hack top from coconut. Pour out milk and scoop out some of the coconut meat, and grate it. (Reserve excess for cookies, custard, cake or whatever you're concocting next week.)
2) Combine chicken stock, coconut milk, Vermouth, soy sauce and curry powder in a double boiler.
3) Gradually add cornstarch, stirring constantly until sauce thickens. Add Naked Chicken and grated coconut, blending well.
4) Pour mixture into preheated coconut shell. Replace hacked-off top and bake in preheated 350° oven about 15 minutes.

2 servings, to be savored at twilight overlooking Charlotte Amalie harbor.

* See page 75

IX

H'UNCLE SAMUEL

Uncle Samburgers and the like

It was in the year of 1917, shortly after the United States had purchased St. Thomas from Denmark (along with the nearby islands of St. Croix and St. John) that I posed for the most celebrated cartoon of the century. The artist had the good fortune to make my acquaintance on the British island of St. Kitts, where we both chanced to be vacationing, and he told me he had searched the globe for someone with my distinguished good looks, to no avail. He implored that I be his model.

I graciously consented and, donning a *Cha Cha Hat* appropriately decorated with red, white and blue flowers, posed for him on the black sands of Basse Terre.

When he had finally placed the finishing touch on his work, he stepped back to scrutinize it, then smiled and waved his drawing pen with a flourish.

"And now for a name!" he said. "A name suited to the image of the United States."

I stroked my beard and pondered for a moment.

"How about utilizing the initials—'U.S.'?" I ventured. "For instance . . . S for Smith?"

The cartoonist slowly nodded his head in approval.

"Excellent," he agreed. "Smith has a nice ring to it. Now all we need is an equally apt first name . . . Upton? Ulric? Or—"

"Ulysses!" I interrupted.

By this time a crowd had gathered.

"Mike 'im H'English!" chirped a pale weazened man with a handle-bar moustache. "For h'example . . . U for 'Ubert . . . and S for Snoddgrass. That w'y the bloke will h'always be h'identified with 'is H'English 'eritage."

He bowed to the waist, then drew himself up to his full height.

"H'allow me to h'introduce myself, Guvnors. Samuel's the nime. Never did 'ave no sirnime. But 'ere on St. Kitts they call me H'Uncle. H'Uncle Samuel."

Without pausing for a reply he strolled off and away, then plunged into the sea and vanished beneath the rippling waves.

"U for Uncle!" a voice called

"And S for Samuel!" piped another.

"Sammy!"

"Sam!"

"UNCLE SAM!" the crowd shouted in unison.

And thus, unbeknownst to historians, the renowned character was conceived.

In celebration, I in turn created a masterpiece in my own right, the heretofore unpublicized:

UNCLE SAMBURGER

(This simple but glamorous dish, with its Yorkshire pudding topping, is a far cry from today's hamburger. It goes without saying that it is appropriate for Fourth of July. But Mad Thinkers everywhere should bear in mind that it should also be featured on lesser known holidays such as "Be Kind To Your Kangaroo Day.")

2 tablespoons butter or mar-
    garine
1 pound lean ground beef
$1/2$ cup onion, chopped
$1/4$ cup green pepper, chopped
$1/4$ cup mushroom stems,
    chopped
1 tablespoon parsley,
    chopped
1 teaspoon worcestershire
$1/4$ cup dry white wine
    salt and pepper to taste

1) Preheat oven and baking casserole at 400°.
2) Melt butter in frying pan and fry hamburger quickly, so that meat stays in quite large chunks, until lightly browned.
3) Push meat to one side; reduce heat and saute onion and green pepper.
4) Stir onion, pepper and meat together and add mushroom stems, parsley, worcestershire and wine. Set aside.

Yorkshire Topping

3 eggs
1 cup milk
  pinch of salt
1 cup flour, unsifted

1) Combine eggs, milk and salt. Beat with a fork until foamy; gradually beat in flour until smooth.
2) Remove hot casserole from oven, and with a slotted spoon quickly remove meat mixture and distribute in baking dish.
3) Pour egg mixture over meat, and tilt to spread evenly.
4) Return to oven and bake, uncovered, about 25 minutes until puffy and well browned.
   4 to 6 servings.

DASHEEN JUMBLE

2 pounds lean ground beef
2 tablespoons olive oil
2 medium-sized onions, finely chopped
2 cloves garlic, minced
1¼ teaspoon salt
¼ teaspoon *each*: nutmeg,
  pepper and oregano
4 cups young dasheen shoots,
  or spinach, chopped
6 eggs

1) Brown beef in oil over high heat. Add onions and garlic, reducing heat, and stir until onions are soft.
2) Add salt, nutmeg, pepper and oregano.
3) Stir in dasheen, or spinach, and cook 5 minutes longer.
4) Add eggs and stir over still lower heat until they are set. Serve at once.
   6 to 8 servings.

HAMBURGER HUMBLE

1 cup onion, chopped
4 cloves garlic, minced
2 tablespoons green pepper,
  chopped
4 tablespoons oil
1 pound lean ground beef
1 teaspoon chili powder

¹/₂ teaspoon salt
Pastry for 9-inch pie plate
1 egg, beaten
1 cup grated cheddar

1) Sauté onion, garlic and green pepper in oil. Add meat, chili powder and salt.
2) Spoon into pastry shell.
3) Blend egg and cheese and spread over meat.
4) Bake 25 to 30 minutes in 375° preheated oven; 40 minutes if pan is pyrex.

Use store bought pastry shell, or as I do, follow this superb recipe for:

PASTRY

2 cups sifted flour
1 teaspoon salt
2 teaspoons double-acting
    baking powder
¹/₂ cup butter or margarine
1 egg
2 tablespoons vinegar
4 tablespoons ice water

1) Sift together flour, salt and baking powder. Cut in butter with pastry cutter or 2 knives.
2) Beat the egg lightly and combine with vinegar and water. Stir into flour-butter mixture, adding more water if needed to make dough softer.
3) Form into a ball and roll out on floured board, about ¹/₄ inch thick (the pastry, not the board) and press into a 9-inch pan.

PENNY IN POCKET

1 tablespoon olive oil
¹/₂ medium onion, sliced thin
¹/₄ cup green pepper, chopped
1 pound lean ground beef
¹/₂ teaspoon salt
¹/₂ teaspoon monosodium glu-
    tamate
¹/₄ teaspoon garlic powder
1 tablespoon parsley, minced
¹/₂ cup cold water
1 tablespoon catsup
¹/₄ pound cheddar cheese,
    sliced

1) Preheat oven to 350°.
2) Grease 1½ quart casserole with olive oil. Combine beef and remaining ingredients except onions and cheese.
3) Spread half of mixture over casserole bottom.
4) Place half of the cheese over this; add a layer of onion.
5) Add remainder of beef mixture and top with rest of cheese.
6) Bake 45 minutes in preheated 350° oven.

BUCCANEER BALLS

 ³/₄ pound ground beef
 ³/₄ cup toasted breadcrumbs
 ¹/₃ cup onion, minced
 ³/₄ teaspoon cornstarch
    pinch of allspice
  1 eggl lightly beaten
 ¹/₄ cup milk
 ³/₄ teaspoon salt
 ¹/₄ cup oil
  3 tablespoons flour
  2 cups water
  1 cup and a splash more of
    burgundy
  2 bouillon cubes
 ¹/₄ teaspoon pepper

1) Combine first 7 ingredients and half the salt.
2) Shape into buccaneer-size balls. About 10.
3) Brown balls in oil, a few at a time. Set aside and drain on paper towels.
4) Blend flour with fat remaining in frying pan. Stir in water, burgundy, bouillon cubes, remaining half of salt, and pepper. Blend until smooth.
5) Simmer balls in sauce 30 minutes.
   4 to 6 servings, depending on whatever else you're concocting.

DASHEEN MEATBALLS

  1 pound ground beef
 ¹/₂ cup dried breadcrumbs
 ¹/₂ cup grated Parmesan
    cheese
  1 egg, beaten
  3 tablespoons dasheen
    leaves, or spinach,
    minced

3 tablespoons parsley,
    minced
3 tablespoons onion, minced
1 teaspoon monosodium glu-
    tamate
1/2 teaspoon salt
1/4 teaspoon pepper
2 tablespoons olive oil

1) Combine all ingredients except olive oil.
2) Shape into 12 meatballs and brown in oil. Remove and set aside.

The Sauce

1) To juices remaining in frying pan add:

4 tablespoons flour
1 8-ounce can tomato sauce
1 teaspoon worcestershire
1 cup beef stock, or 1 cup
    water and 1 beef bouil-
    lon cube

2) Simmer for at least 30 minutes.
3) Add meatballs and continue simmering 30 minutes longer.

TRINIDAD MEAT LOAF

1 1/2 pounds ground beef
1 11-ounce can condensed
    chili beef soup
1/2 cup onion, chopped
1/2 cup toasted breadcrumbs
1 egg, lightly beaten
1 teaspoon chili powder
1/2 teaspoon salt
1/2 cup cheddar cheese, shred-
    ded
1/4 cup tomato, peeled and
    chopped
1/4 cup green pepper, chopped

1) Combine beef, soup, onion, breadcrumbs, egg, chili powder and salt.
2) Place firmly into a 10-inch deep baking dish and bake in preheated 350° oven for 1 1/4 hours.
3) Top with cheese, tomato and green pepper and place under broiler for one minute, or until bubbly.

Pass bowls of: sliced ripe olives, minced onion and bird or chili peppers.
6 servings.

GROUND BEEF CURRY

    1 large onion, chopped
    1 tablespoon butter or mar-
        garine
1 1/2 pounds ground beef
    2 tablespoons cornstarch
1/2 cup stock
    1 teaspoon salt
1/8 teaspoon garlic powder
1/8 teaspoon monosodium glu-
        tamate
    1 tablespoon curry powder
    1 tablespoon lime or lemon
        juice

1) Sauté onion in butter and push to one side of frying pan.
2) Shape meat into bite-size balls (26 to 30) and brown in remaining butter, adding more if needed.
3) Remove meatballs from pan and set aside.
4) Gradually blend cornstarch with stock and simmer in same pan, stirring constantly. Stir in salt, garlic powder, monosodium glutamate and curry powder. Keep on stirring until sauce thickens. Add lime or lemon juice.
5) Place meatballs in sauce and simmer 30 minutes.
   4 to 6 servings. With rice, of course.

MUSAKABOO

    2 tablespoons butter or mar-
        garine
    3 onions, chopped
1 1/2 pounds lean ground beef
    1 tomato, peeled and
        chopped
    2 tablespoons parsley,
        minced
1/2 teaspoon dried basil
1/4 cup dry white wine

3 eggplants, medium-sized
6 tablespoons cracker crumbs
2 egg yolks
2 egg whites
1 cup milk
1/4 cup Parmesan cheese, grated
salt and pepper to taste

1) Melt butter and fry onions until golden brown.
2) Add meat, tomato, parsley, basil, salt, pepper and wine. Cover and simmer until most of liquid has been absorbed.
3) While this cooks, peel eggplants and cut into slices about 1/2 an inch thick, and fry in butter until brown.
4) Butter casserole and sprinkle sides and bottom with cracker crumbs.
5) Place layer of eggplant on bottom.
6) Put meat in mixing bowl and add 3 tablespoons cracker crumbs and egg whites, lightly beaten. Mix well.
7) Cover layer of eggplant with layer of meat mixture and repeat, ending with eggplant.
8) Beat egg yolks and add milk and half the grated cheese, blending thoroughly. Pour over eggplant and dot with butter. Sprinkle with remaining cheese.
9) Bake at 400° in preheated oven, for 1 hour.
6 to 8 servings.

FIG LEAF ROLL-UPS

1 pound ground beef
1 pound lean ground pork
1 large onion, chopped
1 green pepper, chopped
1 teaspoon salt
1/4 teaspoon pepper
4 tablespoons oil
3 tomatoes, peeled and
chopped
1/2 cup raisins
1 tablespoon vinegar
12 ripe olives
4 to 6 young fig leaves*
3 cups grated corn
2 tablespoons butter or margarine
raw wild honey

1) Combine meat, onion, green pepper and seasonings.
2) Brown in oil, then add chopped tomatoes, raisins, vinegar and olives.
3) Wipe fig leaves and simmer in water until they are pliable.
4) Crush the corn and moisten with a little salted water.
5) Spread softened butter on fig leaves and place a layer of crushed corn, then a layer of meat mixture on each.
6) Roll and fold over the ends of the leaves. Tie or skewer with sea egg spines or toothpicks and simmer in water for 1 hour, covered.
7) Remove cover, drizzle with honey and place under broiler until golden.

*Substitute cabbage leaves, if you must.

JAMAICA JUG-JUG

4 pounds chuck roast
1 cup onions, chopped
2 cloves garlic, minced
4 tablespoons lime juice
1/3 cup soy sauce
3 tablespoons worcestershire
2 tablespoons cornstarch
4 potatoes, quartered
1/2 cup water
4 to 6 tablespoons oil

1) Place meat in covered dish or plastic bag. Add onions, soy sauce, garlic, lime juice and worcestershire. Shake well.
2) Refrigerate mixture at least 3 hours, or overnight, turning several times.
3) Drain meat, saving the marinade.
4) Blot dry with paper towel and coat meat with cornstarch, shaking off excess.
5) Heat oil in heavy saucepan over medium-high heat. Brown meat, then lift out and set aside.
6) If needed, add more oil to pan and saute potatoes until golden.
7) Remove potatoes and replace meat in pan; pour reserved marinade over it, and water to cover. Simmer 1 hour or more until tender, but still firm. Return potatoes to pan and cook until tender. About 30 minutes.
6 to 8 servings.

SLAP FOOT STEW*

1/4 pound salt pork, minced
2 pounds stewing beef
1 tablespoon flour
1/2 cup onion, chopped
4 cloves garlic, minced
1 cup beef stock, or 1 cup
    water and 1 bouillon
    cube
1 8 ounce can tomato sauce
1/2 teaspoon coarsely ground
    pepper
1/4 teaspoon ground cloves
1/4 cup parsley, minced
1 bay leaf
6 medium-sized potatoes,
    quartered
6 carrots, quartered
1/2 cup celery, finely chopped
1/2 cup dry white wine
    salt to taste (be wary, as
    beef stock may be salty)

1) Sauté salt pork very slowly. Turn to lowest heat and
   forget it.
2) When pork is tried out, brown beef in drippings, then
   sprinkle it with flour and add onion, garlic, beef stock,
   tomato sauce and remaining seasonings.
3) Place meat in a Dutch oven and simmer covered for 3½
   to 4 hours, until tender. Discard bay leaf.
4) Meanwhile, cook separately until nearly tender: potatoes, carrots and celery.
5) Add vegetables to meat in Dutch oven during last 15
   minutes of cooking.
6) Add white wine 5 minutes before serving. Better still,
   add wine, remove Dutch oven from stove. Chill, and
   leave in refrigerator overnight. The flavor, like me, will
   mellow with age.
   6 to 8 servings.

*Slap Foot Wacky Blacky's favorite

HONDURAS ZIPPAROO

1½ pounds *each*: boneless beef
    chuck and boneless pork
    shoulder cut in 1 inch
    cubes

3 tablespoons olive oil
1 green pepper, chopped
2 cloves garlic, minced
6 medium-sized tomatoes,
    peeled and chopped
1 4-ounce can green chiles,
    seeded and chopped
1/2 cup parsley, minced
1 teaspoon sugar
1/4 teaspoon ground cloves
2 teaspoons ground cumin
1 cup red wine
1 cup beef stock, or 1 cup
    water and a bouillon
    cube
    salt to taste

1) Brown meat and push to side of frying pan. Add vegetables and saute until soft.
2) Add remaining ingredients and simmer about 2 hours, covered. Remove cover and simmer 45 minutes more.
   6 to 8 servings.

BEERY BEEF

3 pounds lean chuck or rump
    of beef
2 tablespoons bacon drip-
    pings or cooking oil
6 large onions, sliced
4 cloves garlic, minced
1 1/2 cups beef stock
2 cups beer
2 tablespoons light brown
    sugar
1/2 teaspoon thyme
1 1/2 tablespoons cornstarch, or
    arrowroot
2 tablespoons wine vinegar
    salt and pepper to taste

1) Cut meat into slices 1 1/2 inches thick and 4 inches long, 2 inches wide.
2) Brown in bacon drippings or oil in frying pan and remove to Dutch oven.
3) Brown onions and garlic and sprinkle over beef.
4) Add stock and boil over high heat until reduced to 1 cup; scrape loose all particles from browning operation and pour over meat.

5) Add beer to cover, sugar and thyme. Cover and set over low heat or in a 325° preheated oven. Cook 2 hours. Cool, and refrigerate overnight.
6) Skim fat. Cook about 30 minutes longer. Blend in cornstarch gradually and add vinegar.
6 to 8 servings. Superb a month from now, frozen. Sacrebleu! Don't serve it frozen! Defrost and serve sizzling hot.

SEVEN HOUR SWEET 'N' SOUR

1 3-to-4 pound round steak
1/4 cup prepared mustard
1/4 cup red currant jelly
1 package dried onion soup
    mix

1) Spread a sheet of heavy duty aluminum foil in baking dish. Use enough foil to wrap steak tightly.
2) Trim fat and place steak on foil. Smear with remaining ingredients on all sides.
3) Fold aluminum foil over steak, making sure the package is very tightly sealed.
4) Place in preheated 250° oven. Take off for Coki Bay and swim and snorkel for seven hours. Then come home and unveil your succulent steak.
Servings? Well. How big an appetite did that swimming and snorkelling create?

CHEESY CHOPS

4 pork chops
2 tablespoons flour
1 tablespoon oil
1/3 cup cheddar cheese, grated
4 medium-sized potatoes,
    sliced thin
2 medium-sized onions,
    sliced thin
3 beef bouillon cubes dis-
    solved in 1 cup boiling
    water
1 tablespoon lime juice
1/4 teaspoon pepper
    salt to taste

1) Trim excess fat from pork chops, sprinkle with flour and brown in oil.
2) Sprinkle 1 tablespoon of cheese over chops.
3) Cover with potato slices, add onion, another tablespoon of cheese, bouillon cubes dissolved in water, lime juice, salt and pepper.
4) Sprinkle with remaining cheese and cover. Simmer 35 to 40 minutes.
   4 servings.

PORTLY PORK

1 4-to-5 pound pork loin roast
salt, pepper and soy sauce
3/4 cup dried apricots
3/4 cup dried prunes
1 cup port, or more

1) Have butcher crack bone and cut almost through into chops.
2) Season with salt, pepper and soy sauce.
3) Combine apricots, prunes and port. Cook fruit-wine mixture uncovered 10 to 15 minutes, or until fruits are plumped. Mix with a spoon and combine well.
4) Stuff fruit into cuts between chops, then tie the roast back into shape, pulling string tightly.
5) Insert meat thermometer, place pork on rack in roasting pan and pour any remaining wine over it.
6) Roast at 325° 3 to 3 1/2 hours, until meat thermometer registers 170°. Splash on some more port now and then.
   6 to 8 servings.

PORK CHOPS SIR FRANCIS

6 pork chops
salt and pepper
3 tablespoons butter
3/4 cup onion, sliced
1/2 teaspoon garlic powder
1/8 teaspoon thyme
1 bay leaf
3/4 cup dry white wine
1 cup sour cream
1 tablespoon paprika

1) Trim fat from chops. Sprinkle meat with salt and freshly ground pepper, and saute in butter.
2) Add onion, garlic powder, thyme and bay leaf, and sauté over medium heat until chops are golden brown on both sides.
3) Reduce heat and add wine. Cover and cook half an hour.
4) Remove chops to a casserole and keep warm.
5) Simmer liquid until reduced by half. Discard bay leaf.
6) Add sour cream and paprika and heat thoroughly, but *do not boil*. Pour sauce over meat. Be sure it's hot.
   6 servings.

MANGO GLAZED HAM

    5 pounds cooked boneless
      ham
      whole cloves, for studding
    2 teaspoons prepared mus-
      tard
$^{1}/_{4}$ cup chopped mangos
$^{1}/_{2}$ cup brown sugar
$^{1}/_{4}$ cup raw wild honey
    1 teaspoon lime juice
    1 teaspoon fresh ginger root,
      grated, or $^{1}/_{4}$ teaspoon
      powdered ginger
$^{1}/_{4}$ cup sweet Vermouth

1) Preheat oven to 325°. Remove gelatin from ham (if canned) and score ham in 1 inch squares.
2) Stud with whole cloves, and brush with mustard.
3) Glaze with mixture of mangos, brown sugar, honey, lime juice, ginger and Vermouth.
4) Bake 1$^{1}/_{2}$ hours, and baste with ardor during the last half hour of baking.
   8 to 10 servings.

POW PORK CHOPS

    1 tablespoon oil
    6 loin pork chops
      salt and pepper to taste
    2 cups orange juice
$^{1}/_{2}$ cup sherry
    2 tablespoons dry onion soup
      mix

1) Heat oil in skillet; add pork chops and brown on both sides.
2) Drain off excess fat and sprinkle chops with salt and pepper to taste. Add orange juice, sherry and soup mix. Cover and simmer 30 to 40 minutes.
6 servings.

BARBECUED RIBS

4 or 5 pounds fresh pork
    spareribs
1 bay leaf
1 onion, sliced
1 celery stalk, sliced
12 peppercorns
1 teaspoon salt
1/2 teaspoon liquid smoke

1) Parboil ribs in enough water to cover. Add all the above ingredients except liquid smoke, simmering until tender and fat slips off when you poke it.
2) Refrigerate overnight. Drain, rub with liquid smoke and cover with barbecue sauce.

Barbecue Sauce

1 teaspoon dry mustard
1/2 cup brown sugar
1 cup tomatoes, peeled and
    chopped
1/2 cup catsup
    pinch red pepper
1 tablespoon raw wild honey
1 tablespoon soy sauce
2 tablespoons dried onion
    soup mix
1 tablespoon oil
1/2 cup vinegar
1 clove garlic, minced

1) Simmer all of the above at least half an hour.
2) Pour over ribs and bake in preheated 350° oven for 2 hours, basting occasionally.
Four generous servings.

MARINATED LAMB RACK

1 8-rib lamb rack
1 medium-sized onion,
    chopped
1 clove garlic, minced
1/2 cup red wine
1/4 cup olive oil
    salt, pepper and monoso-
      dium glutamate
2 teaspoons chopped fresh
    mint or 1/4 teaspoon dried

1) Place lamb in shallow pan or bowl. Mix remaining ingredients and pour over lamb.
2) Cover and marinate several hours, or overnight, refrigerated, turning occasionally.
3) Remove rack and place on grill or spit of rotisserie. Roast 45 to 60 minutes over medium coals, basting frequently with marinade.*
4 to 8 servings.

*If electric grill is used, time according to manufacturer's directions.

Serve with either of
these sauces:

MANGO SAUCE

Peel and slice fruit and simmer 20 minutes in just enough water to cover. Add 1 tablespoon butter or margarine, 1 teaspoon brown sugar, 1/4 teaspoon cinnamon and 1 teaspoon lime juice. Cook until all water has boiled away.

PAPAYA SAUCE

Peel and seed a green papaya and cut into thin slivers. Put in double boiler and cover with cold water. Add 1 tablespoon lime juice, 1 tablespoon sugar, 1/2 teaspoon fresh ginger, grated, or a pinch of powdered. When all water has boiled away, mash fruit with fork. Add more sugar and lime juice to taste.

EROTIC EXOTIC LAMB

3 pounds boneless lamb, cut
    in ¹/₂ inch cubes
1 teaspoon coriander
1 teaspoon chili powder
1 teaspoon cumin
¹/₂ teaspoon saffron
1 teaspoon fresh grated gin-
    ger or ¹/₂ teaspoon pow-
    dered
3 cloves garlic, minced
2 teaspoons salt
1 cup wine vinegar
4 tablespoons oil

1) Roll lamb in mixture of coriander, chili, cumin, saffron and ginger. Sprinkle with minced garlic and salt.
2) Place the above in bowl and pour vinegar over it. Marinate at least 3 hours, or overnight, refrigerated.
3) Remove meat from marinade; blot on paper towels, then brown in oil.
4) Add water to cover and cook over low heat for 30 minutes, or until tender.

LIVER SLIVERS

1 pound calf's liver
1 tablespoon cornstarch
1 teaspoon sugar
2 tablespoons sherry
2 tablespoons soy sauce
3 spring onions
2 tablespoons oil

1) Sliver liver into 1¹/₂ inch slices.
2) Soak for 1 minute in boiling water to seal outside layer. Strain off all water.
3) Remove liver with slotted spoon and mix with cornstarch, sugar, sherry and soy sauce.
4) Cut onions in 1 inch sections.
5) Stir-fry in hot oil for 1 minute. Add spring onions and continue to stir-fry for 2 minutes.
6) Add all remaining ingredients and cook for 2 minutes longer. Serve with steamed rice.
    4 to 6 servings.

BLARNEY STONE TRIPE

3 pounds honeycomb tripe
1 quart milk
6 onions, thinly sliced
1 bay leaf
   salt and pepper to taste
2 tablespoons butter or margarine
3 tablespoons flour
1/4 pound salt pork, or 4 slices
   bacon

1) Wash tripe and simmer 2 hours in a large saucepan or Dutch oven.
2) Drain and rinse in cold water.
3) Cut tripe into pieces about three inches long by one inch wide. Return to saucepan and add milk, onions, bay leaf, and salt and pepper.
4) Melt butter in another saucepan. Add flour and stir constantly for one minute. Strain milk off tripe and add very gradually to butter-flour mixture, blending and stirring for about 2 minutes or until mixture is thickened and smooth.
5) Pour sauce over tripe and onions and discard bayleaf. Simmer over low heat for 15 minutes.
6) Mince salt pork or bacon and fry slowly until golden. Drain on paper towels and sprinkle over tripe. Serve with new boiled potatoes in their jackets.
6 to 8 servings.

SOUSE

2 pounds pigs' feet or jowls
   juice of 5 limes
1 large onion, sliced thin
1/4 cup sweet pepper, chopped
   freshly ground black pepper and salt, to taste
2 medium-sized potatoes,
   diced

1) Scrub pigs' feet or jowls well and cut into small pieces.
2) Soak in pan of cold water to cover for 30 minutes.
3) Bring to a boil and pour water off.
4) Sprinkle with lime juice and cold water to cover and refrigerate overnight.

5) Simmer gently for one hour, or until tender. Skim off fat. During last 15 minutes of cooking add thinly sliced onion and sweet pepper. Salt and pepper to taste.
6) Thicken gravy with 2 potatoes, diced, and serve separately.

X

THE LAMENTABLE DEMISE OF EZ KOFFYAY

His soups live on

All the world knows that the French-Canadian chef, Ez Koffyay,* was renowned throughout Quebec for his masterful soups. But not everyone may be aware that prior to his untimely decease during the blizzard of 1882, he spent several weeks at a winter resort in Bar Harbor, Maine. Ez loved an audience, and Grandpere Antoine had the good fortune to be among a select group of international chefs invited to join a cooks' tour to Maine, the purpose of which was to observe Ez Koffyay in the process of perfecting his latest creation, "Alphabet Soup."

The cooks arrived at the height of the storm, and it was so cold that the shivering guests remained bundled in their thick woolen coats, hats, earmuffs and galoshes as they huddled in the drafty kitchen to watch Ez Koffyay perform.

The dapper little man was dressed as always in an immaculate white uniform and starched chef's hat. He rolled out his special dough and hand-carved each letter of the alphabet in quadruplicate. Then he commanded Zeke, his lanky six-foot-five assistant, to fill a giant copper cauldron with broth.

"Have patience," he announced to the gathering, "for later, as a grand climax to my performance, I shall disclose to you my secret ingredients."

He stood on tiptoe, raising the tray of hand-carved letters up to the boiling brew. But he was so short that his arms could not reach the top of the cauldron.

---

*The phonetic similarity to Escoffier, the illustrious French Chef, is mere coincidence.

"Eh bien, Zeke! Apportes-moi une chaise! Celui-la. Vite!"
he called, pointing to the only chair in the kitchen.

Zeke brought the rickety wooden chair and steadied it
while Ez Koffyay climbed upon it and stood, balancing
himself.

"Et maintenant, les lettres!" he said, gesturing toward the
platter of hand-carved letters.

Zeke handed him the platter and Ez Koffyay, with the
finesse of a master craftsman and performer, slid the letters
into the boiling soup. And as he did so the chair teetered.
The chef tottered.

"Eek, Zeke," he shouted. Then he tumbled head first into
the soup. Whirling about in the boiling brew, Ez Koffyay
groped for the letters he needed and hurled them up to the
surface.

A-U S-E-C-O-U-R-S! he spelled in French, for he knew
not a word of English.

But Zeke knew not a word of French. He stared
dumbfounded at the message. What was the great chef trying
to tell him? *What should he do?*

Meantime, down in the broth, Ez Koffyay struggled
desperately. He had almost given up hope when he
remembered a nautical term he had learned from one of the
seafaring natives of Bar Harbor. He grabbed three letters and
thrust them upward.

S-O-S!

Zeke understood the message at a glance and ran to the
boathouse for a lifeline. But alas, when he returned it was
too late. Ez Koffyay, stewed by the boiling brew, had
breathed his last. A blissful smile upon his face, he reposed
at the bottom of the cauldron.

Grandpere Antoine and the other visiting cooks stared,
shocked and disbelieving, into the mammoth pot.

"A pity."

"A grave tragedy."

"A disaster."

"The recipe for Alphabet Soup is lost to posterity."

"What is there to live for?"

Then one of the cooks jumped feet first into the steaming
cauldron.

One by one, the other cooks jumped into the pot after him.
All, that is, save Grandpere Antoine. Sadly reaching for a
ladle, he dipped it into the broth. Blew. Sipped. To his

horror, it tasted strongly of stale rubber. For in their distress, the cooks had forgotten to remove their galoshes.

Which proves that:

✦✦✦
✦
✦ TOO MANY COOKS' GALOSHES SPOIL THE BROTH ✦
✦
✦✦✦

That afternoon, the tears streaming down my cheeks, I created the following *chef-d'oevre* IN MEMORIUM:

GOULASHA SOUP

2 pounds stewing beef, cut
   into medium-sized cubes
salt and pepper to taste
1/2 teaspoon monosodium glutamate
2 tablespoons butter or margarine
4 large onions, diced
3 green peppers, diced
3 tablespoons paprika
1 tablespoon sugar
1 large 1-pound 12-ounce can
   tomatoes
1/2 teaspoon garlic powder
8 medium potatoes, diced
8 frankfurters, cut into bite
   size pieces

1) Sprinkle beef with salt, pepper and monosodium glutamate.
2) Melt shortening in Dutch oven and brown meat.
3) Add onions and saute until tender.
4) Add green pepper and saute lightly.
5) Add paprika, salt, pepper, sugar, tomatoes, garlic powder and water to cover.
6) Simmer until meat is tender, about 2 to 2¹/₂ hours, adding water as needed.
7) Add potatoes and simmer until tender.
8) Add frankfurters and simmer 5 minutes more.
   8 servings.
   This may be made a day or two ahead of time, for like all stews and people, it will improve with age.

To my great fortune, Ez Koffyay bequeathed to me his immortal recipe for fish chowder, which I proudly share with you.

EZ KOFFYAY'S FISH CHOWDER

1/8 pound salt pork, minced
    very fine
 6 large onions, sliced paper
    thin
 6 large potatoes, sliced paper
    thin
  shaker of flour
3/4 quart milk
 2 pound sturdy fish (haddock
    or cod type)
  salt, pepper and monoso-
    dium glutamate to taste

1) Place minced salt pork in Dutch oven and try out slowly over lowest possible heat. *Do not allow to brown.*
2) Sauté onions and potatoes together in tried out salt pork, stirring constantly.
3) When almost tender (about 10 minutes, but no more) pour in enough water to barely cover them, then sprinkle generously with flour, a very little at a time, stirring constantly to avoid lumping.
4) Now add milk, a very little at a time, continuing to stir constantly for 3 or 4 minutes, until thickened to a creamy consistency.
5) Turn heat very low and simmer gently for 10 minutes or so until potatoes and onions are tender but not mushy.
6) Add fish and simmer about a half an hour longer, until it falls apart into chunky pieces. Add salt, pepper and monosodium glutamate until the flavor is superb. I've watched Ez Koffyay create his masterpiece and although he won't admit it, he sneaks in a few drops of lemon juice at the very last.
7) Pour into heated chowder bowls and serve with pilot crackers and dill pickles.
    4 to 6 servings as a main course, or 8 to 10 as a first course.

And now I offer a sampling of my superb soups, presented to the cooks'-tour-cooks at Bar Harbor.

CREAM OF TANNIA SOUP

6 tannias, peeled and diced
$^1/_8$ cup butter
$^1/_2$ cup scallions, chopped
4 tablespoons flour
1 large can evaporated milk
   salt and pepper to taste
   chopped parsley

1) Drop tannias into boiling salted water to cover.
2) Place butter in frying pan and sauté scallions, but *do not brown.*
3) Add flour and stir well, then add milk very gradually, blending to a smooth paste.
4) Mash drained tannias (reserve cooking water) or put through a potato ricer.
5) Combine with sauce. Add cooking water, salt and pepper.
6) Sprinkle with chopped parsley after spooning into well heated bowls.
   6 to 8 servings.

DASHEEN SOUP

1 tablespoon butter
1 pound dasheen leaves, or
   spinach, chopped
3 cups well seasoned stock
1 teaspoon lime juice.

1) Melt butter in a heavy saucepan. Add greens and simmer, stirring now and then, until leaves are tender.
2) Add stock and continue simmering until rather thick.
3) Sprinkle with lime juice and serve in well heated bowls.
   2 to 3 servings.

WATERCRESS SOUP

4 cups Naked Chicken* stock
$^1/_4$ cup watercress
$^1/_2$ cup minced onion
2 tablespoons mashed potatoes
2 tablespoons light cream
   white pepper and salt to
   taste

1) Bring stock to a boil. Reduce heat.
2) Snip watercress leaves from stems. Leaves should remain whole, stems chopped very fine. Reserve some of the leaves for garnish.
3) Add watercress, onion and mashed potatoes to stock, blending well. Simmer, covered, 20 minutes. Remove from heat and stir in cream.
4) Pour into heated bowls or cups and float a watercress leaf on each.

   4 to 6 servings.

* see page 91.....

CREAM OF PEANUT SOUP

2 tablespoons butter or margarine
2 tablespoons flour
1 quart milk, scalded
1/4 cup celery, chopped fine
1 onion, chopped fine
1 ounce sherry
1 cup peanut butter
1/4 cup chopped peanuts

1) Make a roux of the butter and flour.
2) Stir in the scalded milk very gradually and blend until smooth. Add celery and onion.
3) Add peanut butter gradually and continue stirring until mixture is thoroughly blended.
4) Add sherry just before serving and stir well. Salt to taste.
5) Pour into very hot bowls or cups and sprinkle each serving with the chopped peanuts.

   4 to 6 servings.

MOUNTAINTOP LENTIL SOUP

1 cup dried lentils
8 to 10 cups water
4 tablespoons butter or margarine
1 cup onion, chopped
3 cloves garlic, finely minced
2 crushed bird peppers or a
   pinch of cayenne
4 teaspoons curry powder
1 or more teaspoons salt, to
   taste
2 teaspoons lime juice
   sprinkling of sherry

1) Wash lentils and discard any imperfect ones. Soak in water to cover overnight. Drain well.
2) Boil lentils in 8 cups water, and cook at least an hour until they're mushy. Hold the salt until lentils are cooked.
3) Melt butter in a skillet and add onions and garlic. Saute until yellow.
4) Add bird peppers or cayenne and curry powder. Mix well and saute 3 minutes over very low heat, stirring constantly.
5) Stir onion mixture in with lentils. Now add salt to taste. (The reason for the delay in salting: legumes tend to toughen when boiled in salted water.)
6) Cook about half an hour longer, or until mixture is thoroughly blended. Add lime juice and a sprinkling of sherry, just before serving.
   6 to 8 servings.
   Enjoy on Mountaintop on a windy January night.

CARIB PARTY CHOWDER

1 cup onion, chopped
2 cloves garlic, finely minced
2 cups fresh mushrooms, halved
1 teaspoon fresh chervil, crushed, or 1/4 teaspoon dried
4 tablespoons butter or margarine
2 cans condensed cheddar cheese soup
1 can cream of celery soup
1 soup can water
1 pound scallops, raw
1 pound shrimp, shelled and deveined, raw
1/2 cup dry white wine

1) Sauté onion, garlic, mushrooms and chervil in butter until tender.
2) Stir in soups very gradually, then add water, a little at a time. Keep stirring.
3) Add scallops and shrimp and simmer for 5 minutes. Then add wine and simmer 5 minutes more. *Do not overcook.*
   8 to 10 servings.

CRABBY AVOCADO SOUP

2 large, very ripe avocados
2 tablespoons lime or lemon
   juice
1 clove garlic, finely minced
5 cups Naked Chicken stock
1 cup cooked crabmeat

1) Place avocado, lime juice, garlic and one cup of Naked
   Chicken stock in a blender and whirl until smooth, or
   put mixture through a ricer or wire sieve.
2) Very gradually add remaining stock and blend until
   mixture is creamy. Chill, covered, for at least an hour.
3) Pour avocado soup into chilled bowls and top with
   crabmeat. Garnish with lime wedges.
   6 to 8 servings.

XI

GRISELDA, EMPRESS OF UG

About time for breakfast?

It was my great-great-great aunt, Hermione Bonaparte, who discovered the journal. She was in the attic one rainy day, smoking her corn cob pipe and rummaging through some old love letters when she came across it. The only known biography of Griselda, Empress of Ug.*

Lamentably, as Hermione was scanning the papers, an ash fell from her pipe, setting them aflame, and the strange story might have been lost to posterity were it not for the fact that Aunt Hermione, with her retentive memory, was able to recount it to her third cousin, Gauloise, Le Monsongeur, who committed to writing his illustrious version of the legend. The document, bequeathed to me by Grandpère Antoine, reads as follows:

> "From the moment she could talk, Griselda lay in her cradle, brooding. And the subject of her concern was the age-old riddle: Which came first? The chicken? Or the egg?
>
> " 'No chicky? No eggy? No eggy? No chicky?' she babbled to the rhythm of the rocking cradle.
>
> "By the time she had attained womanhood and become Empress of Ug, Griselda's plump corsetted body took on the proportions of a hen. Her nose was beak-sharp, her laughter shrill, and she surrounded herself with chickens of every fowl description who pecked and clucked and strutted their way through the castle.
>
> "And eggs were everywhere!

*It is interesting to note that although Griselda was reputedly a half sister-in-law of Hermione's grandfather, Napoleon, there is no mention of the Empress in the official Bonaparte geneology.

"One morning the Empress awoke from a profound sleep shrieking, 'THE CHICKEN! The chicken came first! My ESP —my Eggstra Sensory Perception—has revealed it!'

"She called forth the imperial chef, Sav Arin,* to announce, 'In the interest of eggology, I command that from now on all eggs must eggspire. Eggs, and eggs eggsclusively, shall be consumed at my banquet table.

"Eggs, your Highness? Eggsclusively?' the bewildered chef stammered.

"'Eggsactly!' The Empress wagged a clawlike finger. I eggspect you to carry out my wishes with eggsactitude. Let me be eggsplicit. You must eggsperiment, eggspressing your culinary talents with the creation of eggseptional recipes.'

"'But, your ladyship, how can . . .'

"'No eggscuses!' Griselda snapped. 'Disobey my orders and you will be eggscommunicated. Nay, eggsecuted. I do not eggsaggerate. There will be no eggstenuating circumstances. Follow my wishes eggsplicitely or . . . you will cease to eggsist.!'

"Thus having spoken, Griselda's cackling laughter resounded throughout the Empire.

"Chef Sav Arin, his life at stake, rose to the challenge, and it is to his credit that Griselda pronounced his creations, 'Eggsquisite—*Eggsquise!*'

"In 1813, when she passed away at the age of twenty-three (due to malnutrition) she had succeeded in obliterating all eggs from her empire and, to her horror, the entire chicken population as well. To quote her plaintive dying words, 'No eggy?? . . . . No chicky.'

"Be that as it may.

"Small wonder, is it not, that my half-sister was lovingly known to her subjects as:

THE EGGSCENTRIC EMPRESS OF UG

Signed: N. Bonaparte
Elba

April 1, 1815"

Thanks to Hermione Bonaparte and Gauloise, Le Monsongeur, it is my pleasure to share with you Chef Sav Arin's recipes:

---

*Historians have ascertained that he is in no way related to the great French gastronome, Brillat-Savarin.

114

EGGS IN A CLOUD

2 eggs for each serving
1 teaspoon chopped chives,
1 drop tabasco and a pinch
    of basil for each serving
    paprika   salt   pepper

1) Separate egg whites and add chives, tabasco and basil. Beat whites until very stiff.
2) Heap into buttered ramikins and make two hollows, an equal distance apart, not too near the edge.
3) Slip the unbroken egg yolks into the hollows. Sprinkle with salt, pepper and paprika and place ramekins in preheated 350° oven. Bake for 10 minutes, or until eggs are set.

EGGIE SPOOF

1 pound bacon, diced
1 can 1-pound 12 ounce
    solid-pack tomatoes drained
2 tablespoons worcestershire
12 eggs
1/2 cup or more cracker
    crumbs

1) In a large heavy skillet cook diced bacon over a low heat, the slower the better. Drain fat. This can be done the night before, which leaves you free to be a gracious easy-going host the next morning.
2) Add tomatoes and worcestershire. Simmer 10 minutes over very low heat.
3) Beat eggs lightly and add to bacon tomato mixture, then scramble until eggs are soft. Add cracker crumbs to give body, but *do not overcook.*
4) Meanwhile have an assistant making toast. Allow 2 pieces for each serving of Eggie Spoof, and of course extras to pass around.
5) Butter toast and pile Eggie Spoof evenly over 6 whole slices. Quarter the other slice and arrange around Spoof. Serve at once on heated plates.
    6 servings.

HAM FRITTATA

1 cup cooked French-cut
    green beans
1 cup cooked ham, chopped
2 tablespoons grated Parme-
    san
1/2 teaspoon basil
    pinch of garlic powder
1 teaspoon worcestershire
6 eggs, lightly beaten
    green onions, tomatoes,
    ripe olives

1) Combine beans, ham, cheese, basil and garlic and heat
   in large double boiler. Add worcestershire.
2) Add eggs and cover. Cook over low heat for 15 minutes,
   or until eggs are set.
3) Garnish with tomato wedges, green onions and ripe
   olives.
   4 servings.

AUNTY PASTO'S SHIRRED EGGS

(Beanpole's favorite)

4 strips of bacon, diced
3 large tomatoes, halved
1 sweet pepper, minced
1/4 cup grated Parmesan
    cheese
1/8 teaspoon:olive oil, worces-
    tershire, butter, sherry;
    and a sprinkle of garlic
    salt and powdered ore-
    gano for each serving
6 eggs
    butter
    salt

1) Fry bacon slowly and discard fat.
2) Sauté tomato halves in smallest possible amount of
   bacon fat remaining in pan.
3) Brush 6 ramekins lightly with paper towel dipped in
   bacon fat and place a tomato half in each ramekin.
4) Sprinkle each tomato half with remaining ingredients,
   then slide in the eggs. Dot with butter and sprinkle
   lightly with salt.
5) Place in a baking pan in about 1/2 inch water, covered,
   and bake until set. 10 to 15 minutes.
   6 servings.

FIESTA DOMINICO

1 pound bacon, diced
1 tablespoon butter or mar-
    garine
1 cup onion, chopped fine
1/2 cup sweet pepper, sliced
    very thin
1 4-ounce can green chili,
    seeded and chopped
6 large tomatoes, peeled, or 1
    1-pound 12-ounce can
    drained. Reserve liquid.
1/4 teaspoon garlic powder
1/2 teaspoon salt
6 to 8 eggs
    English muffins, halved
    and buttered

1) Sauté bacon until browned, very, very slowly. Remove
with slotted spoon and pour off fat. Place bacon on
paper towels to drain.

2) Wipe residue of bacon fat from pan with paper towels.
Melt butter in same pan and sauté onion, sweet pepper,
and chilis.

3) Add bacon, tomatoes, 3/4 cup of reserved tomato liquid,
garlic powder and salt. Simmer, uncovered, about 30
minutes, or until most of the liquid cooks away.

4) Pour into a baking dish, or distribute in 6 or 8 ramekins.
Make indentations spaced well apart in baking dish, or
in center of each ramekin mixture.

5) Break eggs, one at a time, into a custard cup and slip
into indentations in sauce. If in baking pan, start with
outside edge, placing center egg last.

6) Cover and cook in a 325° oven until eggs are set. 12 to
15 minutes. Serve on buttered English muffins.
6 to 8 servings.

BLACK BEANS AND EGGS

1 1/2 cups black beans
    salt and pepper
1 cup onions, finely chopped
2 cloves garlic, minced
1 bay leaf and a pinch of
    basil
1 cup cheddar cheese, shred-
    ded
2 tablespoons sherry
6 eggs

117

1) Wash black beans, drain, and soak in water to cover overnight, refrigerated.
2) Bring to a boil and simmer, covered, for about 2 hours, or more, until tender.
3) Now add salt, pepper, onions, garlic, bay leaf and basil. Remove from stove and let stand at least 3 hours. Or cool and refrigerate overnight again. Go to the sea and have a moonlight swim.
4) Back to the beans. Warm them up and mash well with a fork. If they don't mash easily, cook them some more until they do. Then stir in cheese, lower heat and stir again until cheese melts. Add sherry.
5) Distribute beans in 6 ramekins. Make a hollow in center of each and slide an egg into each hollow.
6) Bake in preheated 350° oven about 10 to 15 minutes, until eggs are firm.

6 servings.

Delectable in its own right, but even more so served with:

'ERBIE'S HERB BREAD

(the creation of H'Uncle Samuel's twin brother, 'Erbert)

¹/₄ **pound butter or margarine**
¹/₄ **cup each: green onions,**
    and parsley, chopped
    very fine
pinch of tarragon
a foot or more of French
    bread

1) Let butter or margarine soften an hour or so at room temperature. Then mash together with herbs.
2) Slice bread in 2-inch chunks, cutting within ¹/₂ inch of bottom crust.
3) Spread generously with herb butter mixture, between each of the slices.
4) Place on ungreased cooky sheet, sprinkle with a few drops of water, and bake along with Black Beans and Eggs.

ST. BARTS SCRAMBLE

2 tablespoons butter or margarine
8 eggs
2 tablespoons *each:* chives
  and parsley, chopped
1 tablespoon ice water
  salt and pepper to taste

1) Heat water in lower part of double boiler and bring to a boil. Lower heat.
2) Melt butter or margarine in top of double boiler.
3) Beat eggs lightly with a fork. Add chives, parsley and ice water.
4) Pour into top of double boiler and cover. Cook about 5 minutes until eggs start to thicken around edge of pan. Stir very gently, so that thickened eggs are transferred to center of pan and uncooked eggs are pushed toward edges. Repeat, until eggs are softly set.
5) Serve on hot buttered toast.
   3 to 4 servings.

CHEESY SCALLOPED EGGS

6 eggs
1/2 loaf white bread cut into
  cubes
1 cup cheddar cheese, shredded
1 cup milk
1 teaspoon dry mustard
1/2 teaspoon curry powder
1/4 teaspoon garlic powder
1 teaspoon worcestershire
1 tablespoon butter or margarine

1) Lightly beat eggs and combine in mixing bowl with other ingredients.
2) Butter a casserole and pour in the mixture. Dot with butter.
3) Bake at 350°, uncovered, for 20 minutes, or until bubbly.
   4 to 6 servings.

HINDU EGGS

6 hard cooked Eggberts
1/4 cup mayonnaise
2 teaspoons soy sauce
1 tablespoon finely minced
    onion
2 teaspoons minced parsley
2 teaspoons curry powder
    cream sauce

1) Cut the eggs lengthwise. Scoop out yolks and mix well with all other ingredients except the cream sauce and curry powder blending well.
2) Spoon into egg white halves, distributing evenly, and let stand several hours, or overnight.
3) Place in a shallow buttered casserole. Cover with the cream sauce and sprinkle with salt and curry powder.
4) Bake in preheated 350° oven about 20 minutes, until bubbly.

Hindu Egg Sauce

3 tablespoons butter or mar-
    garine
3 tablespoons flour
1 cup milk
    smidgeon of salt (watch it,
    as soy sauce has made
    eggs on the salty side)

1) Slowly heat butter or margarine in double boiler until melted.
2) Add flour gradually until you have a smooth paste.
3) Add milk even more gradually, stirring constantly.
4) Stir over low heat 1 minute, then turn heat to medium and bring sauce to a boil, stirring like the Mad One you are. When sauce is thickened, add your soupcon of salt, pour over eggs.

Many years ago, when Sir Arthur Conan-Doyle honored our island of St. Thomas with his presence, the sole reason for his visit was to acquire my heretofore secret bread recipes. Relaxing in my hammock, he wrote his best-selling book, which later became a popular song. You may remember it: "Holmes on the Range."

MANGO BREAD

³/₄ cup raw or brown sugar
¹/₂ cup butter
2 eggs
2 cups sifted flour
³/₄ cup mangos, peeled and
    chopped
1 teaspoon lime or lemon
    juice
1 teaspoon soda
¹/₄ teaspoon salt
¹/₂ cup grated coconut

1) Cream sugar and butter.
2) Add beaten eggs, ¹/₃ of the flour, then mangos and lime or lemon juice.
3) Add remaining flour, soda, salt and coconut.
4) Pour into a greased bread pan and bake 1 hour in 375° preheated oven.
5) Cool on rack before slicing.

ORANGE COCONUT BREAD

4 cups flour
4 teaspoons baking powder
¹/₂ teaspoon salt
¹/₂ cup raw or brown sugar
1 cup ground coconut
³/₄ cup candied orange peel,
    finely cut
2 eggs
2 cups milk

1) Sift, measure and mix all dry ingredients.
2) Add coconut and orange peel.
3) Beat eggs into milk and add.
4) Pour into two greased bread pans. Bake 45 minutes in a preheated 400° oven. Cool on rack before slicing.

BANANA BREAD

¹/₂ cup butter or margarine
1 cup raw or brown sugar
2 eggs
¹/₄ teaspoon salt
1 cup mashed bananas
¹/₂ cup milk
1 teaspoon soda
1 teaspoon vanilla
2 cups flour

1) Cream butter and sugar; add beaten eggs.
2) Sift, measure, and mix dry ingredients except soda; add soda to milk.
3) Add ⅓ of the flour mixture to sugar, butter and eggs, blending well.
4) Add banana pulp and remaining flour, then milk, soda and vanilla.
5) Pour into a greased bread pan and bake 1 hour in preheated 350° oven. Cool on rack before slicing.

ÑAME BISCUITS

¾ cup cooked ñame, or yam
⅔ cup milk
4 tablespoons melted butter
1¼ cups flour
½ teaspoon salt
4 teaspoons baking powder
1 tablespoon raw or brown
    sugar

1) Mash ñame, or yam, while hot. Add milk and butter and allow mixture to cool.
2) Add remaining ingredients, mix quickly, and drop from a tablespoon onto a greased cooky sheet. Bake in preheated 450° oven for 15 minutes, or until golden.

GOLDEN NUGGETS

6 tablespoons butter
2 tablespoons sugar
1 egg
2 cups flour
1 cup grated coconut
1 teaspoon baking powder
2 tablespoons sherry
    milk

1) Cream butter and sugar. Beat in the egg. Add flour combined with coconut and baking powder, sherry, and enough milk to make a thick dough.
2) Form into rough nuggets and place on greased cooky sheet. Bake in preheated 350° oven for about 15 minutes, until they're golden.

ECOLOGY BARS
(Health Fiend's Feast)

GROUP 1:
- 1 cup safflower oil
- 1 cup raw wild honey
- 1 cup molasses
- 2 oranges (juice, pulp and grated rind)
- 4 eggs, beaten

GROUP 2:
- 1 cup soy flour
- 1 cup whole wheat flour
- 2 cups dried milk powder
- 1 teaspoon ginger root, slivered
- 1 teaspoon dried cinnamon powder
- 1½ teaspoon salt

GROUP 3:
- 1 8-ounce package dried apricots, chopped, *or*
- 1 8-ounce package seedless raisins
- 1 cup oatmeal flakes
- 1 cup toasted wheat germ

1) Blend GROUP 1.
2) Mix together GROUP 2 and GROUP 1.
3) Combine GROUP 3 and fold into the above mixture.
4) Pour into greased and floured 10 by 12½ baking pan. Bake in preheated 350° oven for about 35 minutes. Cool on rack for about 10 minutes.
5) When cool, cut into 15 bars. Wrap in foil or plastic wrap and store in freezer until ready for a Health Fiend's Breakfast.

XII

AUNTY PASTO OF FRENCHMAN'S HILL

Beans for Beanpole

My aunt, Signorina Antonia Giovanni di Pasto, is one of the few inhabitants of Frenchman's Hill who is not of French ancestry. Aunty Pasto has let it be known throughout St. Thomas that she is a direct descendant of an Arawak Indian princess and my Cousin Chris, who landed on the island of St. Crox during his western voyage of 1493.

It is also common knowledge that for thirty-seven years my aunt has been "secretly" engaged to my Frenchtown neighbor, Pierre Le Duc. Their love has deepened over the years, inflamed by an ardor that each sustains for the other's cooking. "Butterball" Aunty Pasto has no use for vegetables beyond the pleasure of growing and cooking them. And "Beanpole" Pierre Le Duc has no use for cookies beyond the pleasure of baking them.

Their temperaments are equally in balance. Aunty Pasto is an incessant talker. Pierre is a man of few words. When he is with his beloved Perdita, she talks. He listens—happily freed of the exertion of bothersome chatter.

One day Aunty Pasto, Pierre and I sat under the manzanita tree at Coki Beach, watching black pelicans swooping down upon their prey beneath the sapphire sea. And my aunt talked. For more than an hour her tongue clicked until finally, unable to stand it any longer, I interrupted her.

"Have you by chance not heard the definition of a bore?"

"A bore?" She stared at me, her large brown eyes puzzled.

"A bore," I explained, "is someone who talks about himself when I would like to talk about myself."

Aunty Pasto threw back her head in laughter. Poking the ribs of her betrothed, she asked, "Do I bore you, Beanpole?"

Pierre Le Duc, who is very ticklish, giggled, kicked my aunt in the ankle, and replied, *"Jamais,* Butterball, *ma cherie.* I get a keeeeeeek out of you!"

With such rapport, you may perhaps wonder why Pierre and his bride-to-be have never married. The answer is simple. Deeper than their mutual passion is their devotion to native soil. For we of Frenchtown would not contemplate more than a passing visit to Frenchman's Hill. And vice versa. It would be unthinkable for Aunty Pasto to make her home by the harbor of Charlotte Amalie on the Caribbean side of St. Thomas. And it would be equally unthinkable for Pierre Le Duc to move to the lush green mountains on the Atlantic side of the island. So there you have it. An impasse.

Aunty Pasto inherited Cousin Chris's enthusiasm for Genoese cooking along with his acquired taste for Spanish food. She claims that many of his recipes were recorded in the log of his voyage of 1493. I suspect that sometimes my aunt's volubility exceeds her veracity. Take for example the account of Cousin Chris's landing on St. Croix, which she told to Pierre and me one summer afternoon as we lolled in the shade of her mango tree. These were her words:

"Immediately upon setting foot on the island, hostile Arawak Indians encircled Grandfather Christopher, leering at him with menacing eyes. Aware of their dietary habits, and fearing they might wish to barbecue him, he quickly outwitted them, calling to his chef in the galley of the Santa Maria, 'A gala banquet, Gonzalez! *Rapidamente!'*

"Instantly, Gonzalez, garbed in an immaculate starched white apron and hat, came forth with a platter of caviar and a magnum of champagne. And while the greedy Arawaks slurped and guzzled, waiters in red jackets set a banquet table with solid gold plates, gleaming crystal and a centerpiece of orchids. Grandfather Christopher gestured to the Arawaks to be seated and the repast began."

Aunty Pasto swatted at a fly with a palm frond, then continued.

"The waiters rushed from the galley of the Santa Maria with platter upon platter of delicacies. Nightingales' tongues, partridge, truffle pate, to name only a few. And the grand finale was a marvel: a white frosted *gateau* decorated with stripes of blueberry confiture and red persimmon stars. It was an exact replica of the American flag."

"A replica of the stars and stripes ... in 1493?" I remonstrated.

But Aunty Pasto ignored my comment.

"From that moment on, Grandfather Christopher was revered on the island of St. Crox and the Arawaks catered to his every whim."

Aunty Pasto smiled and fanned herself with the palm frond. "I swear by Moko Jumbie that every word of the story is true."

My curiosity aroused, I requested to see the log, but she protested, claiming it had been bequeathed to her in strictest secrecy. I let the matter drop.

Knowing that, if true, the incident would be of historic significance, some months later I once again asked to see the log. And once again Aunty Pasto refused, her deep brown eyes brimming with tears.

"I beg you to understand my dilemma, dear nephew. Years ago I buried the ship's log under the mango tree." She dabbed at her eyes with a handkerchief and gestured at the very ground upon which we reclined. "Alas, my hiding of the precious document was so successful that I have indeed hidden it from myself. I have tried time and again to dig it up. With no success."

Pierre Le Duc, dozing to the drone of his beloved's voice, muttered. "Precious document ... buried ... lost ... lost from grave ... grave loss."

Slap Foot Wacky Blacky awoke and fell from my shoulder. And beneath the shade of the hibiscus bush Lord Ignoramus brayed:

"EE-Aw! EE-Aw!"

Here are some of Aunty Pasto's tempting recipes:

CHRISTOPHENE

(Substitute zucchini or Italian squash, but if so do not peel.)
1) Peel and halve christophenes and boil in just enough water to cover, until tender.
2) Drain and serve with sprinkling of olive oil, freshly ground pepper and grated Parmesan cheese.

STUFFED CHRISTOPHENES

3 large christophenes
2 cups cooked meat, finely
    chopped
1 medium-sized onion,
    chopped
1/4 cup toasted breadcrumbs
2 tablespoons oil
2 cups tomatoes, peeled and
    chopped
1/4 cup sweet pepper, chopped
2 tablespoons grated Parme-
    san cheese

1) Halve christophenes, and boil 3 minutes.
2) Scoop out pulp. Crush and combine in a mixing bowl
   with meat, onion and breadcrumbs.
3) Sauté the above in oil until light brown.
4) Place mixture in christophene shells.
5) Spread tomatoes and sweet pepper over stuffed christophenes and sprinkle with grated cheese.
6) Arrange in a buttered casserole and bake for 1½ hours
   in a 300° preheated oven.
   6 servings.

ZUCCHINI-TOMATO CHO CHO

1½ cups peeled sliced toma-
    toes, or 1 1-pound 12-
    ounce can tomatoes
1 medium-sized onion, sliced
    thin
4 medium-sized zucchini, or
    2 christophenes, sliced
    1/8 inch thick (about 4
    cups). Do not peel zuc-
    chini, but do peel chris-
    tophenes.
1/4 pound cheddar cheese,
    shredded
1/2 teaspoon salt
1 10½-ounce can condensed
    cream of celery soup
4 cups cornflakes, crushed, to
    make 2 cups crumbs
1/2 cup melted butter or mar-
    garine

1) Drain tomatoes and drink the juice.
2) Combine with onion, zucchini or christophenes, cheese, salt and pepper, and stir in celery soup.
3) Pour into 6 individual ramekins or 1½ quart casserole.
4) Mix cornflake crumbs and butter or margarine, and sprinkle over vegetable mixture.
5) Bake in preheated 375° oven. About 45 minutes for zucchini. An hour for christophenes.

PAPAYA AU GRATIN

1 medium-sized papaya
4 tablespoons butter
5 tablespoons flour
¼ cup grated cheddar cheese
2 cups milk
½ cup breadcrumbs
   salt and pepper to taste

1) Peel and slice papaya, cover with salted water; bring water to a boil and cook 2 minutes.
2) Combine butter, flour and cheese. Add milk very gradually, stirring constantly over a low heat until sauce thickens.
3) In a greased casserole alternate layers of papaya and cheese sauce, ending with sauce. Sprinkle with breadcrumbs and dot with butter.
4) Bake in preheated 350° oven 15 to 20 minutes.
   2 to 4 servings.

PAPAYA MISHMASH

Peel and split papaya and remove seeds. Boil in salted water to cover until tender. Mash and season to taste with butter, salt and pepper.

BREADFRUIT COO-COO

1 breadfruit
1 cup cooked ham
½ cup water
2 sprigs thyme and parsley
   salt to taste
   pinch of dry mustard

1) Boil, peel and pound the breadfruit.
2) Mince the ham, and chop the thyme and parsley.
3) Mix all ingredients and place in saucepan, stirring until all liquid is absorbed.
4) Press into a greased casserole and place in warm oven until serving time. Dot with butter.
   2 to 4 servings, depending upon size of breadfruit.

FOO-FOO

4 to 5 green plantains
squeeze of lime juice
salt to taste

1) Simmer plantains in water without salt.
2) When soft, peel them, cut into small pieces and pound in a wooden mortar with a pestle or foo-foo pounder. Dip the pestle in cold water frequently to prevent plantains from sticking. Keep pounding until they become a smooth paste.
3) Season to taste with salt and lime juice.

DASHEEN SAUTÉ

2 tablespoons vegetable oil
1 clove garlic, finely minced
1 pound young dasheen
    sprouts, or spinach
1 teaspoon sugar
1/2 teaspoon monosodium glu-
    tamate
2 tablespoons sherry
1/8 teaspoon salt

(This can be prepared in a heavy skillet, but a wok is better.)

1) Heat skillet or wok and add oil.
2) Add minced garlic and cook until very light brown.
3) Add dasheen leaves or spinach. Turn heat to high and stir-fry for 1 minute.
4) Sprinkle the sugar and monosodium glutamate over greens. Stir well, then add sherry and salt.
5) Cover skillet or wok and cook 1 minute longer.

SPINACH IN COCONUT MILK

1 cup grated coconut
1 cup milk
2 pounds spinach
1 teaspoon lime juice
1 onion, sliced thin
1 teaspoon salt
2 bird peppers, crushed, a
   pinch of cayenne or $1/2$
   teaspoon freshly ground
   black pepper

1) Combine coconut and milk in saucepan. Bring to a boil.
2) Remove from heat and let stand for half an hour.
3) Press all the liquid from coconut and discard pulp.
4) Wash and drain spinach. Combine with lime juice, onion, salt, pepper and coconut milk. Simmer 10 minutes.

   4 to 6 servings.

OKRA FUNGI

$2^1/2$ cups boiling water
$1^1/2$ cups corn meal
  2 tablespoons shortening
12 young okras
$1/4$ cup cold water
   salt to taste

1) Cut okra into small pieces and add to boiling water. Turn heat low and simmer 10 minutes.
2) Gradually add cornmeal, blended with $1/4$ cup cold water. Stir until mixture is smooth. Add shortening.
3) Remove from fire and shape into balls about 3 inches in diameter.

   4 to 6 servings.

SPINACH MELANGE

$2^1/2$ pounds spinach
$1^1/2$ teaspoons salt
  2 tablespoons butter or margarine
  2 eggs, lightly beaten
  1 cup milk
$1/8$ teaspoon nutmeg
  1 tablespoon grated onion
$1/2$ cup cheddar cheese, shredded

1) Cook spinach 2 minutes, drain and chop.
2) Mix with remaining ingredients and pour into a shallow 1 quart baking dish.
3) Bake uncovered in a preheated 325° oven 30 to 40 minutes.
6 servings.

POTATO CURRY

4 potatoes, sliced
1 onion, sliced
1 teaspoon vinegar
1 teaspoon curry
1 cup water
1 tablespoon butter or mar-
    garine
salt to taste

1) Sauté potatoes and onion in butter or margarine until golden.
2) Add water, vinegar and curry, and simmer until potatoes are tender. About 15 minutes.

YAM PIE

1 pound yams, cooked
2¹/₂ tablespoons butter or mar-
    garine
¹/₄ cup milk
3 tablespoons grated onion
    breadcrumbs
salt and pepper to taste

1) Mash yams and combine with butter or margarine, milk and onion. Salt and pepper to taste.
2) Place in a greased pie dish.
3) Sprinkle with crumbs and dot with butter.
4) Bake at 450° for 20 minutes.

CONFUSED TOMATOES

4 tablespoons butter or mar-
    garine
4 tomatoes, peeled and
    chopped
2 onions, minced
3 cloves garlic, pulverized
¹/₄ teaspoon powdered ginger

¹/₄ teaspoon ground chili
1 tablespoon coconut, shred-
    ded
¹/₂ teaspoon salt
¹/₂ teaspoon monosodium glu-
    tamate

1) Melt butter or margarine in saucepan.
2) Add onions, garlic, ginger and chili.
3) Sauté 5 minutes, stirring constantly.
4) Add tomatoes, salt, monosodium glutamate and coconut.
5) Simmer for 15 minutes, or until liquid is absorbed.

CARROT WINOS

8 medium-sized carrots
2 tablespoons butter or mar-
    garine
¹/₂ cup green onions, sliced
1 tablespoon water
¹/₄ teaspoon salt
4 teaspoons flour
¹/₂ cup milk
¹/₄ cup white wine
1 teaspoon minced parsley

1) Slice carrots wafer thin.
2) Heat butter or margarine in heavy skillet with tight
   cover, and add sliced carrots and green onions. Saute 4
   minutes. Add water and salt, and simmer until carrots
   are almost tender. About 6 minutes.
3) Sprinkle with flour and stir constantly until flour is
   bubbly.
4) Lower heat and gradually stir in milk and wine until
   thickened.
5) Sprinkle with parsley.
   6 to 8 servings.

BEANPOLE'S BEANEROLE

1¹/₂ pounds fresh green beans,
    slivered, or 3 10-ounce
    packages frozen French
    cut beans
2 cans water chestnuts,
    drained and sliced

1 can bean sprouts, drained
1 can cream of mushroom
    soup
1 cup crumbled French fried
    onion rings.

1) Cook green beans until tender.
2) Layer ingredients and top with french fried onion rings.
3) Bake in preheated 350° oven for about 30 minutes, or
   until it bubbles.
   8 to 10 servings.

ONIONS BAKED IN FOIL

1 large onion for each serv-
    ing

1) Cut small cone-shaped piece from center of top and
   throw into your *pot-au-feu*.
2) Fill *each* hollow with the following:

¹/₄ teaspoon vegetable oil
    pinch of oregano
3 drops tabasco

3) Fill remainder of space with about 1 teaspoon soy sauce.
4) Wrap in foil tightly and bake 1 hour at 450°.
   (Aunty Pasto always bakes potatoes at the same time. Why
waste the oven space? And baked at that high temperature
the potatoes are less starchy. Besides, this oven combination
gives her time to admire me as I cook the steaks.)

OKRA AND TOMATOES

1 tablespoon butter or mar-
    garine
1 cup onion, chopped
1 pound okra, sliced
1 cup tomatoes, peeled and
    chopped
salt and pepper to taste

1) Melt butter or margarine and sauté onion until tender.
2) Add okra, tomatoes, salt and pepper, stirring fast. *Do not
   cook more than 5 minutes.*

133

CREAMED ÑAME

2¹/₂ to 3 pounds ñame, or yams
4 tablespoons flour
¹/₂ cup milk powder
4 tablespoons butter or margarine
¹/₄ cup parsley, chopped
¹/₄ cup scallions, chopped

1) Wash ñame and quarter, for easier handling. Peel and dice into bite size pieces and drop into cold water as you dice. Drain.
2) Place in boiling salted water and cook until tender. About 30 minutes. Drain, reserving 2 cups cooking water for the sauce.
3) Mix flour, milk powder and butter to a smooth paste and add hot water gradually until all is used. Stir constantly until smooth.
4) Bring to a boil and stir in parsley and scallions.
5) Pour over cooked ñame and place in a heated baking dish. Keep hot in medium oven for half an hour. Must be hot to be good.

XIII

SLAP FOOT WACKY BLACKY: OF USE AT LAST!

Strictly for the rabbits

SLAP FOOT WACKY BLACKY
SHE BE SOME USE AT LAST
TOSSEEN UP SALAD
FIT FOR KING'S REPAST.

Whenever I trip over my knock-kneed, pigeon-toed, cross-eyed cat, Slap Foot Wacky Blacky, I question the purpose of her existence. For it would seem that her one goal in life is to provoke trouble.

Take for example my fishing net. Whenever I spread it out to mend it in the shade of the jacaranca tree, she pounces down from a high branch and claws vigorously, purring like a diesel engine. Is it any wonder there are more holes than net?

As for our fishing trips on the *Cha Cha Chug*, all Slap Foot Wacky Blacky does is sleep, rock the boat, or upset the fish bucket. But even though she's more hindrance than help, I permit her to select the choicest yellowtail for her own.

Could it be that I spoil her?

One day we returned from Aunty Pasto's garden on Frenchman's Hill with a basketful of lettuce, scallions, green peppers, tomatoes, avocado pears, parsley and thyme. As usual, I rode on Lord Ignoramus with Slap Foot Wacky Blacky perched on my shoulder, and when we reached Charlotte Amalie we stopped at Lucy's market for salt, freshly ground pepper and a bottle of oil.

Once home again in Frenchtown, I arranged the vegetables attractively in a large earthenware bowl and, just as I had finished, Slap Foot Wacky Blacky, in pursuit of a

135

fly, leapt from my shoulder. She swatted, missed her victim, then wackily untrue to cat tradition, landed on her back in the salad bowl. Uprighting herself with dignity, she proceded to claw at the contents, tearing lettuce into shreds, squirting lime juice and knocking the top from the bottle of oil.

"*Sacre-bleu!* Look what you've done now!" I thundered.

But Slap Foot Wacky Blacky wasn't listening. Ears dowsed in oil, nose wriggling like a rabbit's, she nibbled away at the wreckage until finally, overcome with curiosity, I grabbed a fork, nudged her to one side of the bowl, and sampled the concoction. To my amazement, it was delectable. A masterpiece.

And thus it was that Slap Foot Wacky Blacky chanced to create the original tossed salad.

SLAP FOOT SALAD

Take one knock-kneed, pigeon-toed, cross-eyed cat.
Add:
Any of the ingredients in Slap Foot Wacky Blacky's earthenware bowl: lettuce, scallions, green peppers, tomatoes, avocado pears, fresh parsley and thyme. Or what else do you grow in your garden?

1) Tear greens and throw into the bowl.
2) Chop scallions, mince parsley, slice peppers thin, crumble thyme and discard stems. Add to greens.
3) Quarter tomatoes and set aside to drain.
4) Peel avocado pears and cut into 1 inch cubes. If you are not serving at once, sprinkle them with lime juice to keep them from darkening.
5) Assemble all of the above ingredients and toss lightly with:

Lime Dressing

  3 cloves garlic, halved
¼ cup lime juice
¾ cup light vegetable oil
  1 teaspoon salt
     multiple generous grinds of
        fresh black pepper

1) Place garlic in lime juice and leave for several hours, or overnight. Strain, and discard garlic.
2) Add remaining ingredients and place the mixture in a jar with a tight-fitting lid. Shake long and hard.
3) Pour sparingly over salad, using just enough to lightly coat the greens.

OR

Frenchtown Dressing

1 teaspoon *each*: salt, sea-
    soned salt, dry mustard,
    monosodium glutamate,
    garlic powder, and onion
    powder and mango chut-
    ney (optional)
1 pinch *each*: curry powder,
    tarragon, marjoram,
    thyme
2 tablespoons coconut milk
1 teaspoon mango chutney
    (optional)
1/3 cup malt or wine vinegar
2/3 cup light vegetable oil

1) Mix all dry ingredients and place in a jar with a tight fitting lid.
2) If you don't have fresh coconut milk handy, make some by combining 2 tablespoons packaged shredded coconut and 1/4 cup boiling water. Let stand at least 15 minutes, then strain, reserving juice, and serve the emaciated coconut shreds to your cat, if she'll accept them.
3) Add coconut milk, mango chutney and vinegar to dry ingredients, cover jar tightly, and shake like the manaic you are.
4) Add oil, and shake as above. 17 shakes should do it. Just before tossing over Slap Foot Salad, shake again 7 times.

MANGO CHUTNEY, LORD IGNORAMUS

12 medium mangoes, not too
    ripe
1 large onion, grated
1 cup lime juice
1 1/2 tablespoons salt

1½ cups brown sugar
1 cup raisins, seeded and
    chopped
2 chili peppers, chopped
3 cloves garlic, finely minced
1 tablespoon ginger, shred-
    ded
1½ tablespoons white mustard
    seed
1 cup tamarind pulp
1 cup vinegar

1) Peel and dice mangoes.
2) Combine with other ingredients, except tamarind pulp and vinegar. Let stand overnight, covered.
3) Simmer over very low heat for about 3 hours, stirring frequently. Watch out for scorching. Do not take off for Mountaintop.
4) Peel tamarinds and let pulp and seeds soak in vinegar. Stir to separate pulp from seeds, and discard the latter. Add pulp and vinegar to other chutney ingredients during last hour of simmering.
5) Pack in hot, sterile jars and seal.

CHUCHU SALAD

4 or 5 chuchus (a low calorie
    potato substitute)
1 large onion, chopped
2 tablespoons parsley,
    minced
4 hard boiled eggs, chopped
1 teaspoon worcestershire
    sauce
1 teaspoon lime juice
1 tablespoon olive oil
whisper of garlic powder
dab of mayonnaise
salt and pepper to taste

1) Peel the chuchus and cut into bite size pieces. Drop into 1 inch of boiling salted water and cook until tender. About 20 minutes. The water should all be absorbed, but if any remains, drain.
2) Combine with remaining ingredients and toss lightly. Chill thoroughly.
3) Serve on a bed of lettuce and garnish with tomato wedges, radish curls, parsley sprigs, christophene slivers, and:

GINGERED CUCUMBER

2 large cucumbers
1 teaspoon salt
1½ tablespoons sugar
⅓ cup vinegar
1 teaspoon ginger root,
    minced or ¼ teaspoon
    powdered ginger

1) Peel cucumbers and cut in half lengthwise, then slice crosswise into thin sections.
2) Pour remaining ingredients over cucumbers and stir well so that all are blended.
3) Chill at least an hour.
   6 servings. Or use as garnish.

PAPAYA SALAD

1 medium-sized ripe papaya,
    peeled and cubed
¼ cup sugar
¼ teaspoon paprika
2 tablespoons lime juice
1 teaspoon minced onion
½ cup vinegar
1 cup vegetable oil
½ teaspoon dry mustard
    salt to taste
    lettuce or mixed greens

1) Marinate all ingredients except greens and papaya seeds for at least 30 minutes, then add seeds.
2) Chill for an hour or more, then at serving time toss lightly with salad greens.

PLANTAIN SALAD

Sprinkle quartered plantains, or bananas, with lime juice. Coat lightly with mayonnaise and roll in crushed peanuts. Serve on a bed of shredded lettuce.

MARINATED PEPPERS

Slice sweet peppers thin and marinate in Lime Dressing.* Chill at least an hour before serving, stirring now and then.

LIME MOLD

3 packages lime jello
2½ cups hot water
1½ cups gingerale
¼ cup chopped nuts
1 pound green or tokay
   grapes
½ cup celery, chopped
1 8-ounce can crushed pineapple

1) Add lime jello gradually to gingerale and when blended combine with hot water, stirring to be sure it's smooth.
2) Set aside in refrigerator until partially jelled, then add remaining ingredients, stirring now and then until mixture is not quite firmly set. Pour into 2 molds and chill an hour or so longer.
16 servings.

CUCUMBER MOLD

1 package lime jello
1 cup hot water
1 cup chopped cucumber
1 cup creamed small curd
   cottage cheese
¾ cup mayonnaise
½ teaspoon lime or lemon
   juice
2 teaspoons onion, grated
½ teaspoon soy sauce

1) Dissolve jello in hot water and cool.
2) Combine with remaining ingredients and chill in refrigerator until set.
4 to 6 servings.

AVOCADO PEAR RING

2 tablespoons gelatin
½ cup cold water
1¼ cups hot water
4 tablespoons lime juice
¾ cup chopped celery
1 tablespoon grated onion
2½ teaspoons salt
2 drops tabasco
1 teaspoon worcestershire
¾ cup mayonnaise
3 cups mashed avocado

1) Dissolve gelatin in cold water. Pour in hot water and add lime juice. Allow to partially set.
2) Add remaining ingredients and chill, stirring now and then. Leave in refrigerator for several more hours until firmly set.
6 to 8 servings.

TOMATO ASPIC

3 cups tomato juice
2 envelopes, or 2 table-
        spoons, gelatin
1/2 cup *each:* chopped onions,
        celery and sweet green
        pepper
1 teaspoon worcestershire
        sauce
1 teaspoon lime juice
1 teaspoon sugar
2 drops tabasco
    a whisper of garlic powder,
        oregano and basil
    salt and pepper to taste

1) Bring 2 cups of tomato juice to a boil. Soften gelatin in another cup. Combine, blending well.
2) Add all remaining ingredients and refrigerate, stirring now and then until almost set. Chill several hours longer, until ready to serve.
4 to 6 servings.

BEET MOLD

(a zingaroo with cold roast beef)

1 package lemon jello
1 cup boiling water
3/4 cups canned beet juice
3 tablespoons vinegar
1/2 teaspoon salt
4 tablespoons horseradish
1 tablespoon minced onion
1/4 cup cucumbers, peeled and
        diced
1 cup canned beets, drained
        and diced

1) Sprinkle jello on canned beet juice, to dissolve.
2) Combine with boiling water and chill.
3) Add remaining ingredients and refrigerate several hours, stirring to blend evenly.

CALYPSO CALICO

1 pound sauerkraut, rinsed,
   well drained, and cut
   across a few times for
   easy serving
1 medium onion, sliced paper thin
1 4-ounce can pimientos,
   chopped

Pour over the above:

1/2 cup vinegar
1/2 cup sugar
1/4 cup salad oil
1 teaspoon salt
1/2 teaspoon black pepper
1/2 teaspoon garlic powder
1 teaspoon celery seed

Mix well and marinate several hours. Chill.
6 to 8 servings.

EGGPLANT STUFFED TOMATOES

2 medium-sized eggplants
2 tablespoons onion,
   chopped
1 clove garlic, minced
1/4 cup oil
1 teaspoon lime juice
   salt and pepper to taste
4 to 6 tomatoes
3 tablespoons parsley,
   chopped

1) Place whole unpeeled eggplants in preheated 400° oven
   and bake about 45 minutes, or until tender.
2) Sauté onion and garlic in oil until yellow.
3) Cut eggplant in half and remove pulp. Mash with a fork
   in mixing bowl and add oil, gradually, alternately with
   lime juice.
4) Add onion, garlic, and salt and pepper to taste. Mix well
   and chill, preferably overnight.
5) Halve tomatoes. Scoop out some of pulp and throw it in
   your soup pot.
6) Fill tomato halves with eggplant mixture and sprinkle
   with chopped parsley.
   4 to 6 servings, depending on size of tomatoes.

FRUITY-TOOT

Fresh pineapple chunks,
  thick banana chunks
  dipped in lime or lemon
  juice, papaya chunks,
  mango slices and avoca-
  do pear chunks, dipped
  in lime or lemon juice.

1) Arrange each of the above on long bamboo skewers and place on a large platter, on a bed of lettuce.
2) Pass the:

Macadamia Dressing

1 cup vegetable oil
$^1/_4$ cup lime juice
1 teaspoon grated lime rind
$^1/_2$ teaspoon salt
$^1/_2$ teaspoon dry mustard
$^1/_4$ teaspoon freshly ground
  black pepper
$1^1/_2$ cups macadamia nuts,
  chopped

1) Shake together oil, lime juice, lime rind, salt, dry mustard and pepper, in a tightly covered jar.
2) At serving time, add nuts and shake again. Hard. Dribble a little over skewered fruit and pass the remainder in a bowl.

GARBANZO GUNG-HO

2 16-ounce cans garbanzos,
  drained
$^1/_3$ cup wine vinegar
2 tablespoons vegetable oil
1 tablespoon olive oil
1 teaspoon salt
$^1/_4$ teaspoon freshly ground
  black pepper, 2 crushed
  bird peppers or a pinch
  of cayenne
1 cup onions, chopped
2 tablespoons parsley,
  chopped
1 clove garlic, very finely
  minced
$^1/_4$ cup sweet pepper, chopped
1 teaspoon sugar
$^1/_2$ teaspoon soy sauce

1) Combine all ingredients.
2) Mix well. Chill, preferably overnight.
   About 6 servings.

GARLIC SHRIMP SALAD

3/4 cup lime dressing
   (in this case use 6 cloves
      garlic, halved; with nee-
      dle and coarse string,
      make a garlic lai, and add
      to dressing leaving
      enough extra string to
      hang over edge of jar, for
      easy removal)
1/4 cup ripe pitted olives,
   halved
 1 pound shrimp
   dash of cayenne
   juice of 1 lime
   salad greens
 4 hard cooked eggs, coarsely
   chopped

1) Place lime dressing in a jar. Add olives and chill for at least 3 hours.
2) Cook shrimp in boiling salted water, with a dash of cayenne and a squeeze of lime juice; 3 to 5 minutes, depending upon size of shrimp.
3) Peel and devein. Chill thoroughly.
4) At serving time, tear greens into salad bowl and add shrimp. Remove garlic lai and drizzle lime dressing over salad. Add hard-cooked eggs, and toss lightly.
   4 to 6 servings.

SUNNY SHRIMP SALAD

1/2 cup mayonnaise
 2 tablespoons lime or lemon
   juice
1/2 teaspoon prepared mustard
 1 cup cooked shrimp, peeled
   and deveined
 2 hard-cooked eggs, chopped
 1 cup carrots, coarsely grated
1/2 cup chopped celery
 1 teaspoon celery salt
   crisp lettuce or romaine

144

1) Blend mayonnaise with lime juice and mustard.
2) Stir in shrimp, eggs, carrots, celery and celery salt.
3) Arrange lettuce on plates and distribute the salad evenly.
   6 servings.

CRABMEAT STUFFED TOMATO

  1 cup flaked cooked fresh
      crabmeat, or 1 (6$^{1}/_{2}$
      ounce) can
$^{1}/_{4}$ cup mayonnaise
$^{1}/_{2}$ teaspoon curry powder
  1 teaspoon lime juice
$^{1}/_{4}$ cup finely chopped celery
$^{1}/_{2}$ teaspoon salt
  1 cup cooked rice
  1 cup cooked peas
  4 to 6 large tomatoes
  4 to 6 hard-cooked eggs,
      quartered
    salad greens
    lime wedges

1) Scoop out centers of tomato and throw the pulp into
   your *pot-au-feu.* Turn tomatoes upside down on a plate,
   to drain.
2) Put crabmeat in a bowl. Separate crab pieces and
   remove membrane.
3) Combine all ingredients except tomatoes and greens, and
   mix well.
4) Pile the mixture into hollowed tomatoes, and serve on a
   bed of greens. Garnish with egg and lime wedges.
   4 to 6 servings, depending upon size of tomatoes.

XIV

CARNIVAAAAAAAAAAAL!

A Jumbie Jumble of Festive Fare

AUNTY PASTO DISAPPEAR MYSTERIOUSLY
PIERE SEARCH FOR BELOVED DELERIOUSLY
HE RUN 'ROUN D'ISLAND IN FANATICAL STATE
TO RESCUE FIANCEE FROM PIRATICAL FATE
FEARFUL WHEN HE FIND HER IT MAY BE TOO
LATE.

On the third day of Carnival Aunty Pasto vanished. I was with Pierre Le Duc when he found the crudely printed note taped to the front door of her home.

37 YEARS
TOO LONG TO WAIT.
SO I TAKE YOUR PERDITA
FOR NUMBER 10 MATE.

—BLUEBEARD

"Butterball?" Pierre cried. "Married? . . . To Bluebeard? *Èpouvantable!*"

"Kidnapped?" I suggested.

"Of course. But who would pull such a cruel trick?"

Pierre grabbed the doorknob. Turned. Twisted. Rattled. To no avail.

He rushed to the porch window.

Locked.

To the back door.

Locked.

Every entrance to the house was bolted shut. And all the blinds were down. Strange indeed, for Aunty Pasto's house was always as open as her heart.

The sun had slipped below the horizon when we returned to Frenchtown, but there was still enough light for us to read the note on Pierre Le Duc's door.

146

PERDITA! LOST!
YOUR BELOVED BUTTERBALL
BE MINE ALL MINE
BEFORE D'NIGHTFALL.

—BLUEBEARD

A short masked man dressed as a pirate ran from Frenchman's Bar. His laughter was high and shrill and he raced past us waving a dagger.

"Bluebeard!" Pierre shouted, in hot pursuit. But by the time he reached the harbor the pirate was lost among the crowd of tromping revellers.

In a frenzy, Pierre Le Duc searched St. Thomas for Perdita, his Butterball. He checked Bluebeard's Castle and every other hotel on the island. He roamed the beaches, from Magens Bay to Red Rock. And each night he joined the trompers, vainly hoping to catch a glimpse of his beloved. But the festivities only deepened his grief.

On the day of the grand parade, he bravely carried on with the act he had rehearsed some months earlier. The float showed a jungle scene in the center of which the dejected Pierre crouched in a cast iron pot surrounded by a circle of blacks in leopard skins, pounding on bongo drums.

I, in my role of Mocko Jumbie, preceded the float, and all went smoothly until we reached the judges' stand beside the Grand Hotel.

"Perdita!" a voice shrilled from among the bystanders.

Pierre jumped from the float, knocking me from my stilts and sending me sprawling on Kronprindsen's Gade. He tackled the masquerader and ripped off his mask.

Butterball!

She flung herself into the arms of her lover. "Thirty-seven years!" she sobbed. "Too long, Beanpole. I had to do this . . . to find out . . . to find out if you loved me." She glanced up at me and winked.

The next day, more than a thousand St. Thomians gathered at Coki Beach to watch me give the bride away. The marital vows, composed by Aunty Pasto, read in part:

. . . To love, honor, and obey
And live on Frenchman's Hill
Forever and a day."

To which Pierre assented, "I do."

As they embraced, Aunty Pasto glanced at me over her husband's shoulder, her eyes aglow. And I reflected with pride upon the success of my tutelage, for I had long since indoctrinated her with Grandpere Antoine's philosophy. The first words spoken by my infant aunt had been:

✱✱✱✱✱✱✱✱✱✱✱✱✱✱
✱ THINK MAD ✱
✱✱✱✱✱✱✱✱✱✱✱✱✱✱

Late that night, after the newly-weds had departed for a honeymoon on St. John, I was inspired to create my:

MOCKO JUMBIE JUMBLE

1 16-to-17 ounce can pie
    cherries
1 8.5 ounce can crushed pi-
    neapple
1 1-pound 2.5-ounce package
    yellow cake mix
¼ cup chopped pecans
⅛ pound butter or margarine

1) Jumble up the cherries, pineapple and cake mix.
2) Pour into a greased baking pan and sprinkle with nuts. Dot with butter. Bake according to directions on cake mix package.
3) Cool for at least 30 minutes before serving.

St. Thomians celebrate many holidays throughout the year: Three King's Day, Transfer Day, Easter Monday, Whit-Monday, Organic Act Day, Supplication Day (when we pray that there will be no hurricanes), Thanksgiving Day (when we give thanks that the hurricane season is over and we are still alive), and many, many more. All of these holidays call for festive fare. Even the deeply religious ones. For immediately upon leaving church on Supplication Day and Thanksgiving Day, the parties begin.

FRUITCOOK CAKIES

1 pound candied cherries
1 pound candied pineapple
1 pound chopped dates
1 7-ounce can flaked coconut
1 pound pecans, chopped
¾ cup rum or brandy
3 cups flour
½ cup butter or margarine

1 cup brown sugar
4 eggs
3 tablespoons milk
3 teaspoons baking soda
1/2 teaspoon salt
1 teaspoon cinnamon
1 teaspoon nutmeg
1/2 teaspoon allspice

1) Cut fruits into small pieces and combine with coconut and nuts.
2) Pour rum or brandy over fruit mixture.
3) Sprinkle half of the flour over it and blend. Let it stand.
4) In large mixing bowl, cream butter and sugar until light and fluffy. Add eggs one at a time, beating after each addition.
5) Add milk, soda, salt and spices and blend well.
6) Combine fruit mixture with caky batter; use hands to thoroughly distribute fruit in batter.
7) Drop by teaspoonfuls on a greased cooky sheet. Bake in preheated 325° oven. About 15 minutes.
   About 16 dozen fruitcook cakies. Wrap in foil or plastic wrap and freeze.

RUM HO HOS

30 vanilla wafers, crushed
 2 tablespoons cocoa
 2 tablespoons corn syrup
 1/2 cup nut meats, chopped
 1/4 cup rum
   confectioners sugar

1) Mix first 5 ingredients and form into balls.
2) Roll in confectioners sugar.
3) Store in airtight container and refrigerate. The longer the better.

MACADAMIA MORSELS

1/2 cup butter or margarine
1/8 teaspoon salt
 1 teaspoon vanilla
 1 cup ground macadamia
     nuts
 2 tablespoons sugar
 1 cup sifted cake flour
   confectioners sugar

1) Cream butter; add salt, sugar and vanilla, and blend thoroughly.
2) Stir nutmeats and flour into creamed mixture.
3) Form dough in small marble-size balls, finger shapes, or crescents.
4) Place on a greased cooky sheet and bake 45 minutes in a preheated 350° oven.
5) While still slightly warm, gently roll cookies in confectioners sugar.
About 3 dozen morsels.

PENUCHI NUTS

1 cup brown sugar
1 cup granulated sugar
1/2 cup sour cream
1 teaspoon vanilla
2 1/2 cups nuts, whole or halved

1) Combine sugars and sour cream in a heavy saucepan.
2) Cook over very low heat stirring constantly until mixture reaches a temperature of 246° on a candy thermometer, or forms a fairly firm ball when dropped in cold water.
3) Remove from heat; add vanilla and nuts, stirring until a light sugar coating begins to form on nuts.
4) Turn out on wax paper and separate the nuts into bite size pieces.
About a pound of candied nuts.

DATE NUT BALLS

1 1/3 cups sweetened condensed
    milk (15-ounce can)
1 tablespoon rum
2 cups finely crushed vanilla
    wafers
1 cup chopped dates
1/2 cup chopped nuts
1 cup confectioners sugar

1) Blend condensed milk with rum. Add vanilla wafer crumbs and mix well.
2) Combine dates and nutmeats, then add to first mixture.
3) Sprinkle sifted confectioners sugar over this and knead it in.
4) Pinch off small pieces of dough and roll into balls between palms of hands. When all dough is used, roll

each ball in confectioners sugar. Wrap each individually in foil squares, or layer them in a cooky jar separated by plastic wrap. May be stored in refrigerator or frozen until needed.

About 3¹/₂ dozen date balls.

BANANA FUDGY

1 ripe banana
  milk
2¹/₂ cups sugar
1 teaspoon butter or margar-
    ine
1 teaspoon vanilla
  pinch of salt

1) Mash banana. Add enough milk to make 1 cup.
2) Combine sugar, salt, butter and banana mixture.
3) Boil until thick, or until a drop in cold water forms a ball.
4) Add vanilla and remove from heat. Beat until smooth. Pour into a buttered pan. When set, cut into 1-inch squares.

SEA FOAM CANDY

1 egg white
3 cups light brown sugar
1 cup water
1 teaspoon vanilla

1) Beat white of egg until foamy.
2) Boil sugar and water until it makes a soft ball in cold water.
3) Stir syrup into egg. Add vanilla and drop by spoonful onto oiled paper.

GRAHAM CRACKER LOG

16 or 18 graham crackers (sin-
    gle)
16 large marshmallows, cut
    fine
1 cup chopped nuts
1 cup finely cut dates,
    packed
2 or 3 tablespoons of cream
    or evaporated milk
  candied cherries
  whipped cream

1) Roll crackers into crumbs between two sheets of waxed paper. Place all but 2 tablespoons of crumbs in a mixing bowl.
2) Add marshmallows, nuts and dates. Mix well. Add enough cream to make a soft dough.
3) Form with hands into a log roll.
4) Roll in remaining crumbs, wrap in waxed paper or plastic wrap and refrigerate at least 12 hours.
5) To serve, garnish with candied cherries and a splash of whipped cream.

RAINBOW MOLD

1 3-ounce package *each*:
  strawberry, orange, lemon, lime and grape jello
5 cups boiling water
1¼ cups cold water
2 cups (1 pint container) non-
  dairy whipped topping
½ teaspoon water mixed with
  a drop of green food
  coloring
1⅓ cups flaked coconut
  maraschino cherries

1) Dissolve each package of gelatin separately in 1 cup boiling water. Add ¼ cup cold water to each.
2) Chill strawberry gelatin until very thick.
3) Line a 9 inch spring-form pan with oiled wax paper and cut to extend 3 inches above pan.
4) Whip strawberry gelatin until fluffy and about double in volume. Spoon into pan and chill until set.
5) Meanwhile chill other gelatin flavors in the order listed above. As each thickens, remove it to a bowl and whip it, as with the strawberry. Then layer it in pan. *Do not spoon a layer in until the previous one has set firmly.*
6) Chill overnight. At serving time carefully peel off waxed paper from sides of pan. Place a serving plate on top and quickly invert. Remove bottom of spring form pan and remaining waxed paper.
7) Spread whipped cream over top and sides of mold.
8) Garnish with tinted coconut: mix ½ teaspoon water with a drop of green food coloring. Add flaked coconut and toss with a fork, to tint evenly. Sprinkle over whipped topping.

9) Scatter a few pieces of maraschino cherries over this. Make it gaudy: candied citrus fruit? nuts?*

PINEAPPLE BRULLÉ

1 8-ounce package cream
    cheese, softened
1 cup heavy cream, whipped
1¹/₂ cups crushed pineapple,
    drained
¹/₂ cup chopped nuts
¹/₄ teaspoon ground nutmeg
1¹/₂ cups brown sugar, packed

1) Beat cream cheese with whipped cream. Stir in pineapple, nuts and nutmeg. Turn into a 9 inch baking pan.
2) Sift brown sugar evenly over entire surface. Broil about 5 inches below broiler until sugar melts and begins to bubble. Cool 20 to 30 minutes at room temperature, then refrigerate at least 1 hour, but not more than 4 hours.
3) At serving time, tap the caramel to break it and spoon into sherbet glasses.
    8 to 10 servings.

CRANBERRY SAUCE CAKE

1 1-pound 2.5-ounce package
    white cake mix
1 cup whole cranberry sauce
2 eggs
1 cup water
3 tablespoons grated orange
    peel
1 cup chopped pecans
2 cups confectioners sugar
2 tablespoons butter or mar-
    garine

1) Combine cake mix, ²/₃ cup of the cranberry sauce, eggs, water and orange peel in a mixing bowl. Beat 4 minutes. Stir in the nutmeats.
2) Grease a 13 x 9 x 2-inch baking pan. Sprinkle with flour. Pour in cake batter and bake for 40 to 45 minutes in preheated 350° oven. Remove and let cool 5 minutes.
3) Meanwhile combine remaining ¹/₃ cup cranberry sauce with sugar and butter, and beat until smooth.
4) Spread icing over warm cake. Serve warm or cold.
    12 servings.

RUM CAKE CARNIVAAAAAAAAL!

I

(In 3 Steps)
- ¹/₂ cup butter or margarine
- 1 cup sugar
- 2 eggs, separated
- 1¹/₂ teaspoons grated orange peel
- 2 cups sifted cake flour
- 2 teaspoons baking powder
- ¹/₄ teaspoon baking soda
- ¹/₄ teaspoon salt
- ¹/₂ cup orange juice
- ¹/₂ cup rum
- ¹/₂ teaspoon vanilla

II

Rum Whipped Filling

III

Bittersweet Frosting
- ²/₃ cup chopped pecans
- ¹/₄ cup chopped maraschino cherries

1) Cream shortening. Add ³/₄ cup sugar. Beat in egg yolks and orange peel and continue beating until light.
2) Measure and sift dry ingreadients together.
3) Combine orange juice, ¹/₄ cup rum and vanilla.
4) Alternately add liquid and dry ingredients to creamed butter.
5) Beat egg whites to soft peaks and gradually add ¹/₄ cup remaining sugar. Continue to beat whites until stiff. Fold into batter.
6) Pour into 2 8-inch round cake pans which have been oiled and lined with wax paper.
7) Bake 25 minutes in a preheated 350° oven. Place cakes on racks.
8) When cool, split each cake into two layers. Sprinkle the 4 tops with remaining ¹/₄ cup rum. Spread filling between layers.
9) Cover top and sides of cake with frosting. Sprinkle nuts around top edge and press into sides. Garnish with maraschino cherries.

Rum Whipped Filling

- 1 envelope, or 1 tablespoon, unflavored gelatin
- ¹/₂ cup cold water

2 cups heavy cream
1/2 cup confectioners sugar
1/4 cup rum

1) Sprinkle gelatin over cold water in saucepan. Let soften.
2) Add cream to gelatin.
3) Gradually add sugar, beating slowly. Add rum and cooled gelatin. Whip until stiff, but not buttery.

Bittersweet Frosting

4 squares unsweetened choc-
    olate, melted
1 cup sifted confectioners
    sugar
2 tablespoons hot water
2 eggs
1/3 cup butter or margarine

1) Beat chocolate and sugar together. Gradually add hot water.
2) Gently stir in eggs, one at a time, and continue beating. Add butter and beat until smooth.
3) Spread frosting over top and sides of rum cake, and so back to step 9 above.
Now
   have
      a
     HAPPY
     CRAZY
     WILD
CARNAVAAAAAAAL!
         BE YOU UP IN ALASKA
         OR DOWN TRINIDAD
       KEEP HEART FULL OF SONG
         AND REMEMBER:
          Think Mad

And
  if you've eaten too much
    don't
      go
        away
          mad.

ALEWIFE: White-fleshed fish, good for chowder. Substitutes: porgy, parrot or cod.

BARRACUDA (Bechine): Voracious, pikelike fish. Has a long body, pointed head and vicious teeth.

BIRD PEPPER: Wild cayenne. Substitute: powered cayenne.

BONITA: (LITTLE TUNNY, SPOTTED TUNA): Robust, chunky fish, bluish above and silver beneath. Flesh is coarse and dark. Its roe is a delicacy.

BOBBY BIRD'S EGGS (SEA BIRD'S EGGS): Smaller than pullet's eggs. Delicious hard-cooked, with salt, pepper, a sprinkle of lime juice and Worcestershire.

BREADFRUIT: Roundish or oblong fruit with a tough, yellowish-green bumpy or prickly skin. Its cream-colored flesh is good boiled, roasted or fried.

CALYPSO ENGLISH: West Indian jargon, baffling to tourists, who find it hard to believe its basic words are English.

CHA-CHA-HAT: Tall hat made of palm fronds, usually decorated with colorful straw objects, such as birds, fish, flowers or donkeys. A creation originated in Frenchtown, St. Thomas.

CONCH ("CONK"): Giant molusk with sweet, succulent tough flesh. Delicious raw with a sprinkling of lime juice, or in stews or salad. Its spiral shell is used by West Indian fishermen as a trumpet—for an S.O.S. at sea, or to announce an incoming catch upon landing.

CHRISTOPHENE (CHAYOTE, CHOCHO): Pear-shaped squash, ranging from white to dark green. Its firm, crisp flesh has a delicate flavor similar to summer squash.

CHUCHU: Small white native squash.

CRAWFISH (CRAYFISH, LANGOUSTE): A lobster without claws; first cousin to an African lobster tail.

DASHEEN (CALALOO, ELEPHANT EARS): Leaves of the taro, a tuberous plant root. Substitutes: spinach, turnip or beet greens.

FRENCHTOWN: Small fishing village on the harbor of St. Thomas, U.S.V.I.

FRENCHMAN'S HILL: Lush agricultural French colony on the Atlantic side of St. Thomas.

FUNGI: Cornmeal pudding, with okra. Served with fish.

GENIP: This small round fruit makes a refreshing beverage. Native children who don't have "penny in pocket" for candy pluck genips from the tree, pop the fruit from its leathery skin into their mouths and suck on the "sourball."

GRO-GRO: See Grunt.

GROUPER: Form of sea bass.

GRUNT (GRO-GRO): Derives its name from the noise it makes when removed from the fishhook.

GUAVA: Oval fruit of a tropical evergreen tree. Served raw, stewed, or made into jam, jelly or paste. Delicious with cream cheese.

JUMBIE: See Moko Jumbie.

KINGFISH: Sturdy iron-grey fish. Grows up to five feet long.

LANGOUSTE: See Crawfish.

MAMMEE (MAMMEE APPLE): Fruit with leathery brown skin. The three seeds inside the mammee give it a skull-like appearance.

MAMMEEHEAD: A bald person.

MANGO: A succulent fruit. Better varieties such as Julie, Peter, Bombay or Gordon have smooth juicy flesh, free from fiber. The wild mango, with its pronounced turpentine flavor and stringy flesh, is excellent for chutney.

MOKO JUMBIE: Spirit of Carnival.

NAME: First cousin to a yam.

PAPAYA (LECHOSA): Large melonlike fruit. When ripe, its colors range from yellow to deep orange, with a mass of small blackish seeds.

ST. BARTHOLEMEW (ST. BARTS): West Indian island known for its palm frond weaving. Along with Grandpere Antoine and Grandemere Marie, many of its inhabitants migrated to St. Thomas and established the little fishing village of Frenchtown, where the Mad Hatter now has his domain.

ST. KITTS: British West Indian Island, noted for its black sand beaches.

SEA EGG: West Indian name for the spiny sea urchin.

SOURSOP: Large heart-shaped fruit often weighing up to four or five pounds. Its white cottony pulp surrounds black seeds, and is slightly acid.

TAMARIND: the fruit of the tamarind tree consists of a little brown pod, two to three inches long. This surrounds a sticky acid pulp containing several seeds. The tangy pulp is delicious stewed, or in chutney. Substitute: dried apricots.

TANNIA: A long tuber obtained mostly in the dry season. Its dark brown skin is rough and slightly hairy. A good potato substitute.

TARO: Tuberous plant root. See Dasheen. Substitute: white potato.

UNITED STATES VIRGIN ISLANDS:

ST. CROIX: Largest of the three U. S. Virgins, known for its gently rolling country and colonial sugar-cane plantations.

ST. JOHN: Smallest of the U. S. Virgins. Most of the island is now a United States National Park.

ST. THOMAS: Liveliest and most densely populated—this is where the Action is!

WHELK: Sea snail.

YAM: The West Indian tuber, unlike its orange stateside counterpart, has a tough thick skin and its flesh is often white.

INDEX

165

MY OWN MAD RECIPES